HOW CAN I FIND HEALING?

Also by Jim Glennon

YOUR HEALING IS WITHIN YOU

HOW CAN I FIND HEALING?

by

Jim Glennon

HODDER AND STOUGHTON
LONDON SYDNEY AUCKLAND TORONTO

British Library Cataloguing in Publication Data

Glennon, Jim
   How can I find healing?
   1. Pastoral medicine   2. Pastoral
   psychology
   I. Title
   256'.82   BV4337

ISBN 0 340 34821 6

Hodder and Stoughton Editorial Office: 47 Bedford Square, London WC1B 3DP

For
members of the Healing Ministry Congregation
at St Andrew's Cathedral, Sydney,
who have enabled so many people
to find healing

"He has granted to us
his precious and very great promises"
2 Peter 1:4

CONTENTS

AUTHOR'S PREFACE

I have been very encouraged by the way my earlier book, *Your Healing Is Within You* (1978), has been received and used. It has been well reviewed and widely read. I am encouraged because it means that the principles of the healing ministry that have been developed within our congregation and acted on, day in and day out, have been generally approved by a wider audience, from both the pastoral and theological points of view. It isn't good enough to have a conviction yourself; it needs corporate support from others as well! Part of the satisfaction is that I have no reason to want to alter what was written; it has stood the test of time and is still my position today.

The present book is a sequel to it. It is in two parts and Part I is addressed to troubled people. "What you must know" is a positional paper and is new material. What follows is intended to give simple and sensible guidelines to those who read, so that they know what they need do to put these principles of healing into practice and what they can expect as a result. Part II is for the worker in the healing ministry. Our long and practical involvement in this ministry no doubt means that we have a contribution to make in this area, though, until our recent introduction of residential seminars, we have not ventured to say so. The conclusion is a résumé of the leadership given by the Lambeth Conference on this subject over this century.

It is my pleasure to thank warmly those who have assisted me in any way in the preparation of the manuscript for publication. The title and the idea of the book were suggested to me by Edward England when he was a director of Hodder and Stoughton. I am grateful to him and to my publishers, Hodder and Stoughton, both of whom have always shown a caring and personal interest in their author from "down under". The Australian branch of the firm also has been very ready to assist me and has done a splendid job in promoting and distributing my earlier book in this country.

I would like to take this opportunity of expressing my very warm appreciation of the guidance given me by the Most Reverend Sir Marcus Loane, who, until his recent retirement, was Archbishop of Sydney and Primate of Australia. Both before and during the time Sir Marcus was Archbishop, he allowed me to discuss the healing ministry with him, and I profited very much from his counsel and encouragement. This does not identify His Grace (or anyone else) with all that I have written, but it enables me to say how much I have valued the generous liberty that has been given me by the Archbishop, as well as by the Dean and Chapter, to exercise this ministry in St Andrew's Cathedral, Sydney.

A.J.G.

PART I

GUIDELINES FOR SICK AND WORRIED PEOPLE

1

WHAT YOU MUST KNOW

You have what you affirm

"THEN IT HAPPENED, and it was almost a relief to know it was over," Maudie was telling me.

Five months previously the bedside phone had rung just before midnight. Paul* reached for it, but before he could speak a calm but urgent voice came in. "Is that the Becketts'? ... It's the Cottage Hospital here, Sister Carrington speaking. It's Max – he's had an accident. We don't know how serious it is. The doctor has just arrived. You had better come."

They were out of bed at once, putting on dressing-gowns as they hurried to the car. Maudie felt in the grip of a cold fear and could only repeat, "I knew it ... I knew it ..." Paul was silent as they drove the three kilometres to the local hospital on the outskirts of the town. Max had been out on his motorbike visiting friends. It must have happened on his way home.

They stopped behind the doctor's car in the drive; the ambulance was further up. At first they walked quickly along the verandah, and then more slowly as they came to the ward which served as Casualty, and where they could see light and movement.

Max was lying very still, hardly able to speak and in shock. There was a good deal of blood from the cuts and abrasions where he had hit the road. They waited grimly, hardly daring to speak – it is different when it is one of

---

*All names used in this book are fictitious.

your own. Fifteen minutes later the doctor said, "It's not good, we can't keep him here. I'll get the ambulance to take him to the District Hospital. It's his arm and his leg and there may be internal injuries. I think you should go with him."

Maudie paused as she related her story to me. She and her husband Paul were visiting Sydney during the holiday season, and as many visitors do, had come to the healing service. They had introduced themselves to me during the greeting time, and on hearing something of what had happened to them, I invited them to come and see me. Now we were talking in my room at the Cathedral.

"He wanted a bike," Paul broke in. "You know what it's like; some of his mates had bikes and he wanted one, too."

"I was the one who didn't want him to have it," Maudie went on. "When I was young I knew someone who was killed on a motorbike, and this shocked me deeply – partly because I knew him well, and also because he was a very good rider. I thought that if that could happen to Ted, it could happen to anyone."

"He was twenty years of age," his father continued, "so it had to be his own decision."

"I couldn't get it out of my mind that he might have an accident," Maudie said. "It seemed that the very awfulness of it made it stick in my mind. I dwelt on it, and it became more and more a burden and nightmare."

"I tried to tell her not to worry," Paul came in, "but that didn't seem to help."

"I didn't want to be afraid, of course," Maudie continued, "but the more I thought about it, the worse it became. It was like that for more than twelve months. Then it happened, and . . ."

I thought how distressed she looked as she recalled this harrowing experience. Then she broke and began to cry. It was important for her to express her feelings, and I helped her do this. "It must have been a terrible time for you . . ." After she regained her poise the conversation continued. We finally reached the point where we could review what had been talked about and face up to the fear she had and the problem it makes. They were both able to face this in a positive way, and although there was more to be said, a beginning had been made.

"We've learnt a lot from what we have been through," Maudie said ruefully.

"Yes, I understand. Most of the things I know have been learnt the hard way," I said. "Would you like us to pray about it and believe for God's help at this time? We could pray for Max, too."

They nodded their agreement as Maudie added, "Max is making progress and we are believing for his full recovery ... though it will take time."

"What I dread befalls me"

My own experience of fear and its results has been like this as well. It was just as though I had planned it that way. But, of course, it was the very opposite of what I wanted. What I wanted were things that were good, that made for peace of mind and that enabled me to reach the goals I had for my life. Yet the opposite of what I wanted began to happen – and it wasn't on one occasion only.

To begin with, there was only a slight suggestion that what I was afraid would happen, *was* happening in fact. I didn't see a connection between them at first. But as time went by it became more obvious. It had the effect of confirming my fears – there was a basis for them after all.

To be afraid that something would happen and then to find it actually happening (even if only in degree) made me more afraid. Then more things went wrong. It isn't too much to say that as time went by, it was like the print that is developed from a negative; one reflected the other in detail. I need to say that this was a progressive thing spread over a number of years, and like most things that slowly get worse, you don't realise you are caught until it is too late.

If I couldn't do anything about my fears when they were in an incipient form, I certainly couldn't do anything about them as they grew worse. It reached the point where they would sweep over me and I was powerless to resist. Sometimes it was without warning and without reason. I was becoming paralytic with this problem and the anguish was mounting. Some of the truest words in the Bible are "fear has torment".[1] Only those who have been in the grip of fear can understand the agony of mind it brings.

Sometime ago I visited a clergyman who was dying of cancer and suffering greatly. I had met him only once before. As I took my place by his bedside he said to me, "The only person who can minister to me is someone who has suffered." I replied, "I have not suffered in the way you are suffering, but I have suffered in my mind." He looked at me and said quietly, "I feel I have known you all my life." Deep calls unto deep.

Perhaps I should say that my fears were about people. From my earliest days I have been apprehensive about meeting people whom I did not know: In the long run I was afraid of everyone – some more than others, but everyone. This was irrational of course, but it wasn't any easier to control because of that.

It was not until I reached breaking point that I came to understand the awful truth that fear *brings about* what we fear. Two things brought this home to me. The first was a verse in the Bible, Job 3:25, "The thing that I fear comes upon me, and what I dread befalls me." This, incidentally, was the explanation for Job's troubles – that is what he is saying here.

The second thing is something well known to all Australians. One of the customs of our Aboriginal people in their tribal life is "pointing the bone". The medicine man can point a bone at a member of the tribe, and it means that that man is going to die. As a result of the ritual that has been directed to him, the man has an all-consuming fear that he is going to die. He believes so that he does not doubt in his heart. And so he dies.

I am not saying that every passing fear has this result, or that every experience of sustained fear has this result. That would be too sweeping a generalisation. There are, of course, other reasons that cause accidents and sickness. But, nevertheless, as far as fear is concerned, the general principle that "what I dread befalls me" is what the Bible says, and this is what I am echoing.

This is disconcerting enough, but there is more to follow which affects everybody.

"Faith" for your problem

Whether or not we are fearful, we all have problems of some kind. You tell me yours and I will tell you mine.

There are two things about problems that I would like to refer to. The first is that everyone's problem situation is unique. No two people are the same, and neither are their circumstances. This is what the psychologist calls "the law of individual differences". In passing, this means that the help or ministry that is given to a troubled person is always personal. There is no such thing as everyone receiving a "No. 9 pill" as we used to say in the Army about those who reported sick at the Regimental Aid Post. (I don't think that really happened at the R.A.P., but we liked to say it did!)

The second point is that all troubled people have something in common, and that is, *they are affirming their problem.* You might say that it is inevitable; after all, it is what they have, it is what they see, it is what they are concerned about. It is often given a name and the person is labelled as such, "I am a depressive", or "my marriage is on the rocks", or "I have arthritis", etc.

Although it may be natural to react in those terms, it doesn't alter the fact that this will *perpetuate the problem.* And because it continues, there will be a cumulative effect so that it *worsens.* Irrespective of how it came about, it is now being kept alive because it is being *affirmed* in an on-going way. You see, your faith is what you affirm, and if you are affirming your problem, that is the kind of "faith" you have. Like the Aboriginal who has had the bone pointed at him, *you have "faith" for your problem.*

A good deal of the difficulty lies in the fact that, to begin with, it may not be our fault at all. We may have inherited characteristics that have given us a bad start in some respects. We may be the innocent victim of circumstances that have come upon us. But notwithstanding this, it is also true that if the way we react is keeping things going, then, ultimately, it is a *self-inflicted wound* and the end responsibility is ours.

I said worse was to come, and I haven't finished with that yet. Just as we can keep our own difficulties going, so too can we keep the difficulties going *in other people*, if that is what we affirm about them.

This may seem to be even more incredible, but it is just as true and just as real. The thing that upsets me, perhaps more than anything else, is the knowledge that I can keep, and have kept, other people in their bondage just by reacting to them in terms of the difficulty I see in them. It isn't that I set out to do this; perhaps they have characteristics which "bug" me, and which may be making problems for others. When I see someone being hurt by someone else's faults, I tend to get "up tight". It is so easy to justify one's irritations.

The Bible's continued abhorrence of "the pointing of the finger" and "calling your brother a fool" are expressions of its concern that, by so doing, we are locking people into their personal difficulties. And that is what I have actually found. As long as I react in this way, the person concerned stays in that condition. But when, at last, I react to what they are like in a positive way, so that I am believing something good for them, they are very often released from their bondage and come into a new experience of wholeness.

We are all making this mistake every day, about ourselves and others. And we are so used to it that we take it for granted and almost certainly don't realise the consequences. If we were told about them, we would be incredulous, and even if we wanted to alter our ways it would be difficult. Old habits die hard, and bad habits die harder. Many would affirm that they are only facing the facts and taking a responsible attitude; to do any differently would be to play "the ostrich" and be unrealistic. Yet it is because I am as realistic and have as deep a sense of responsibility as anyone else, that I want to go on record as saying that to react only in terms of the difficulties, either in oneself or in others, is being as short-sighted and destructive as one can possibly be. It is a negative "faith" and brings about a negative result.

Problems and promises

How, then, can we react to our difficulties so that there is a different and better result? The answer to this requires that we understand the origin of our problems and the purpose they serve.

Where do our problems come from?

The story of the Garden of Eden conveys the truth that when God made the world and human kind, he saw that they were good. That is the way God designed things and the way he wanted them to continue. It reveals God's will for us, both then and now; hence Jesus taught us to pray, "Thy will be done, on earth as it is in heaven."[2]

But man wasn't made to be a robot. He was made in the likeness and image of God, and as such has the power of choice. The other thing that the Garden story conveys to us is that man soon started to choose wrongly and step outside the limits that God had placed around him. It says that Satan tempted him to do this and he yielded to the temptation. Sin means "the breaking of the divine law". When that law had been broken once, it was inevitable that it would continue to be broken. Man had fallen from his pristine position, and he has remained like that. He still knows what is right, but so often does what is wrong, and the whole of the human race is affected. The Bible calls it the sin of the world.

All sickness and infirmity are the direct entail of the sin of the world. All forms of disharmony and disease, whether personal or corporate, national, international or cosmic, are the result of man's disobedience to God, and they are the punishment he has brought on himself. It says in the Commandments that the iniquity of the fathers is visited upon the children to the third and fourth generation – there is much more in that than meets the eye. As well as being affected by the sin of the race and that of our fathers, we also sin personally and suffer because of that.

With this in mind, we might now ask: do our problems come from God? When, for example, a child is born deformed or dies of leukaemia, is that what God has sent? Of course not! What sort of God do people who affirm that think we have? He is made out to be an ogre of the most terrible kind. If fallen man did such things, public revulsion would be such that he would be ostracised for life. Yet we can say this about God, who is holy in every respect, and not "turn a hair". It shows the arrant nonsense people can talk when it comes to religion. If our circumstances are different from the perfection of the Most High God, then be assured that they have not come from God, and they are different from his will.

Where, then, do they come from? We can only read what Jesus said and learn from him. After the general group of disciples had been sent out to preach the gospel and heal the sick, the Bible goes on to say, "The seventy returned with joy, saying, 'Lord, even the demons are subject to us in your name!' And he said to them, 'I saw Satan fall like lightning from heaven. Behold, I have given you authority to tread upon serpents and scorpions, and over all the power of the enemy; and nothing shall hurt you.'"[3] Elsewhere it says, "the devil has sinned from the beginning. The reason the Son of God appeared was to destroy the works of the devil."[4]

It is plain from these and many other scriptures that *our Lord saw sickness and infirmity as being the will and work of Satan*, which in turn had been made possible by the fall of man and the sin of the world. To this we have the added and vital information that the purpose of Christ's coming was *to destroy the works of the devil.*

Well might we ask then, what change does this make in our circumstances today? Or is it, as someone has put it, "pie in the sky when you die by and by"?

The promises of God and the will of God

There is no need to say to informed Christians that our Lord pre-eminently destroyed the works of the devil through his crucifixion and resurrection. By the perfect offering of himself on the altar of the cross he took away the sin of the world, so that he was able to say, "It is finished".[5] His resurrection was the proof that Satan's rule had been broken and a new order had been introduced, which he referred to as the kingdom of God. This kingdom is a heavenly and spiritual reality that will be experienced in its fullness only when "the kingdom of the world has become the kingdom of our Lord and of his Christ".[6]

But this same kingdom also has been established in the hearts and lives of those who accept what Christ has done, and it has a "here and now" reality as well. "The kingdom of God is in the midst of you,"[7] Jesus said. The "here and now" kingdom is made up of the "precious and very great promises"[8] that God has made. Put together, these promises are what we call "The New Testament". God's part has been to provide this resource; our part is to search the scriptures so that we know what it is.

The point about the promises that is of special importance is that *they reveal God's will to us in a fallen world.* It is not enough to know God's will as it was revealed in the Garden of Eden when that will has been frustrated by Satan and by man's disobedience. We need a revelation of his will that takes this into account, as it also takes into account the atoning work of Christ. That is exactly what God has done for us in bestowing on us his rich and wonderful promises as set out in the scriptures. They reveal God's will for us in the "here and now" kingdom.

Let us look at some of these promises so that we have an

informed idea of what they are and of their relevance to us.

By way of introduction, let me say that I once took a mission in the parish of Oakey, which is in Queensland near Toowoomba. Good preparations had been made by the rector and other members of the church, and we had a creative and rewarding week together. The church wasn't big enough for the mission services, so we met in the local high school's fine auditorium. After I had been speaking at the meetings for several days, the rector said to me, "I can't help noticing how you have the promises of God at your finger-tips." What he said has remained with me – not because it was complimentary, but because that needs to be a characteristic of all Christians who would pray effectively.

That is why we read the Bible, because that is where the promises of God are set out. We are not so much looking for a text that says this or that, so much as we are wanting to understand the Bible, and the New Testament in particular, in an overall way. What we need to see are the promises of God as revealed in the broad themes of scripture, and to understand any particular verse in that wider context. We are not to understand the promises by a single verse, and we are not to set aside a broad theme of scriptural promise because of an isolated passage, the more so if that passage is open to more than one interpretation.

Well, what are some of the great themes of scriptural promise? The most important, of course, is the remission of sins that God offers to those who believe that Christ died that we might be forgiven. When we accept that forgiveness, we no longer affirm that we are without God in our lives, "because, if you confess with your lips that Jesus is Lord and believe in your heart that God raised him from the dead, you will be saved".[9]

Another of the great themes in the New Testament, in the ministry and teaching of our Lord, in his call and commission to his followers, and in his provision for the church today, is that of healing. This is clearly presented in James 5: 14,15, "Is any among you sick? Let him call for the elders of the church, and let them pray over him, anointing him with oil in the name of the Lord; and the prayer of faith will save the sick man, and the Lord will raise him up . . ." His great and gracious words, "Truly, truly, I say to you, he who believes in me will also do the works that I do,"[10] are to be understood in this context.

Another area of provision that we need to be concerned and clear about is to do with material things. As with everything, balance is important. On one hand, Jesus expressly warned against being preoccupied with building up material wealth and giving it priority over "treasure in heaven".[11] It is so easy to put riches before God and so make a god of riches. On the other hand and given that we have our priorities right, God has promised to meet our material needs so that we have what we eat and drink and wear. (You can't be more materialistic than that.) Jesus said, "If God so clothes the grass of the field, which today is alive and tomorrow is thrown into the oven, will he not much more clothe you, O men of little faith? Therefore do not be anxious saying, 'What shall we eat?' or 'What shall we drink?' or 'What shall we wear?' . . . But seek first his kingdom and his righteousness, and all these things shall be yours as well."[12]

More could and should be said about the range and detail of what God has promised to give. For some curious reason, this theme has not been developed in Christian literature as it should be. There are great books about this subject and that, but there is a dearth of writing that sees the broad canvas as well as the fine detail. Another way of putting it is to say there is no lack of emphasis upon the things of eternity (thank God!), but there is precious little emphasis upon what God wants us to have here and now. My guess is that this is because there is an even more curious lack of understanding that the promises of God reveal the will of God. They either do or they don't – there can be no half measures. My point, clearly and plainly stated, is that the promises of God, as developed in the broad themes of scripture, are God's covenant with us, and that it is his will that we be partakers of them.

It is not so much that there is any soundly based argument that says differently (though there are some theologians who expressly take that position); in my view it is more that we are so used to a watered-down version of Christianity that the matter of God's promises in their range and detail is not seriously considered.

Problems bring us to the promises

So far we have seen something of the problems and something of the promises. Now we are going to tie them together, because they are intimately connected. This is the whole point of this chapter and a large part of the point of this book.

What we are to learn from our difficulties

The clue to understanding the connection between problems and promises is found in the experience of St Paul. He had more than his share of difficulties, and it is worth reading about them: "Five times I have received at the hands of the Jews the forty lashes less one. Three times I have been beaten with rods; once I was stoned. Three times I have been shipwrecked; a night and a day I have been adrift at sea; on frequent journeys, in danger from rivers, danger from robbers, danger from my own people, danger from Gentiles, danger in the city, danger in the wilderness, danger at sea, danger from false brethren; in toil and hardship, through many a sleepless night, in hunger and thirst, often without food, in cold and exposure."[13]

He sums it up when he refers to his experiences in Asia: "We do not want you to be ignorant, brethren, of the affliction we experienced in Asia; for we were so utterly, unbearably crushed that we despaired of life itself. Why, we felt that we had received the sentence of death ... "[14]

My first thought on reading this is to be encouraged by

the fact that St Paul had his problems too. They continued on and had a cumulative effect until he "despaired of life itself". He was at breaking point.

Up to that stage he had only been reacting in terms of his difficulties, but then he put on his theological "thinking-cap". He had been given an "abundance of revelations"[15] and, in a unique way, could see things from God's perspective. When he did this, he realised that there was more to his problems than he first thought. He knew that "all things work together for good to them that love God",[16] which must include the very things that were so hurtful to him. That being so, he then asked the "crunch" question, "What is the good towards which my problems are working?" He knew that, while they came from the devil and the sin of the world, they had also been allowed by God and were therefore serving a purpose of God that was good – because God is good. But what was the "good"?

Then he comes up with the answer: " . . . we believe now that we had this experience of coming to the end of our tether that we might learn to trust, not in ourselves, but in God who can raise the dead."[17] "To trust, not in ourselves, but in God" means that we have been brought to faith – faith in God. And faith in God means, for the Christian, faith in what God has promised. There you have it!

How to react in every circumstance

Once we see this, all our thinking about the difficulties that come our way is transformed. Christ has won the victory over Satan through the cross. God's kingdom has been established and is within you. The purpose of difficulties is to bring us to faith – faith in the promises of God. Suddenly everything hangs together. It makes sense of life. It makes sense of Christianity. And it makes sense (if I may say so with great reverence) of God. We have now a cogent structure of thought to which we will be able to relate all that happens and all that we are to do. It can be rightly called a theology of permitted difficulties.

We can now answer the question that was raised earlier. If reacting to a problem in terms of the problem only perpetuates it and it becomes worse, how can we react in a way that will give a different and better result? The answer is to react to the problem by coming to faith in the relevant promise(s) of God. Then our need is met, his kingdom is extended and his will is done.

To avoid any misunderstanding, we would make the following point with the utmost clarity. We are not to *ignore* the problem; that would be foolish in the extreme. We are to *face* the problem "square on", and to *react* by believing for and bringing to bear the relevant resource that God provides. That, we maintain, is the Christian position.

Let us illustrate this straight away. We began by talking about fear, its torment and consequences. Now we can say that there is no need to react to stress by being afraid because it says in 2 Timothy 1:7 (A.V.), "God hath not given us the spirit of fear; but of power, and of love, and of a sound mind." As far as God is concerned, we do not have to be afraid; fear comes from Satan and the sin of the world. We are to react by coming to faith in the power and love and soundness of mind that God provides. "Love casts out fear."[18]

How well I remember coming to that realisation in my own fear-ridden life. What a tremendous relief and release it was to know that I could stop affirming the problem and start affirming the answer; and to find, not all at once but as time went by, that it worked for me. In the next chapter we will look into detail at how we go about this. At the moment we are concentrating on what we must *know* and, when that has been worked through, we will turn our attention to what we need *do*.

It is worth noting that the passage of scripture quoted above makes it completely clear that it is God's will for us to have healing from fear. Once it is shown conclusively that healing is available in one area, there is a logical and powerful argument for believing it is available in other

areas, especially when it is remembered that fear is an
important factor in many emotional disturbances, and
that emotional factors play such a large part in physical
disorders. It makes all the more credible and relevant the
statement of scripture, "the prayer offered in faith will
make the sick person well."[19]

The meaning of faith

If the concept of coming to faith in what God provides is
to make sense, we have to know what faith means. I have a
lively sympathy for people who see things in terms of what
they are and what they have. After all, the whole of life is
geared that way. So, although we will soon be looking at
faith-in-action, it will be helpful to say something about it
now that will give meaning and insight to what has
already been said.

St Paul tells us that "we walk by faith, not by sight".[20]
The meaning of this is further brought out when we are
told, "Faith is the assurance of things hoped for, the
conviction of things not seen."[21] The Living New
Testament throws further light on our path when it freely
translates that verse as, "Faith is the confident assurance
that something we want is going to happen. It is the
certainty that what we hope for is waiting for us, even
though we cannot see it up ahead."

The problems are what we see. The promises are what
we hope for, "even though we cannot see" them at the
time. We are saying that we are not to affirm the problem
that we see; we are to affirm the relevant promise by faith.

At first hearing, this is both confusing and frustrating.
It just does not seem to make sense. The reaction of some
might even be one of indignation. I well remember what I
thought when this was first said to me in the context of
healing. At the time I had iritis, which is a painful and
serious eye complaint. "But what about my iritis?" I kept
saying. The real point was that I could not see past what I
had and the label that had been put on me. The label was
right as far as it went and the medical treatment was

necessary. And it was also true that as long as that was
what I accepted, I had recurring attacks of iritis. But as I
increased my understanding of what faith meant, so that I
affirmed what I was believing for, rather than what I had,
the attacks became less frequent and less severe until they
finally disappeared completely, never to return.

Faith is not what is happening at the moment. Faith is
being sure about what "is going to happen".

The blessing of Jesus

We also need to understand that the Person of the Trinity
who makes real the promises of God is the Holy Spirit. He
is one of the vital parts of this whole exercise, and we must
understand his person and ministries in a special way if we
are going to draw on the blessings we need. One of his
characteristics, the Bible says, is that he is the Spirit of
Christ, so that, although he is a person in his own right
with his own range of ministries, it is also true that he is
totally self-effacing, so that he takes of Christ and shows
him to us.[22]

This means that, whenever we are drawing on a promise
of God to meet a present need, and however much that
promise is concerned with physical or material things, the
Holy Spirit who communicates that answer to prayer will
always and automatically *take of Christ and show him to
the person concerned*. He has to do that; it is his essential
character. The person praying, or the one being prayed
for, may not have this in mind at all, but that doesn't
matter. If the Holy Spirit is active in ministry, Christ is
being glorified and Christ is being shown to all concerned
in any and every way that is needful.

In practice, it means that, irrespective of what happens
on the physical or circumstantial level, there is always a
blessing of Christ relevant to the circumstances. To the
one who is already a Christian, the blessing will be a
deepening of his spiritual life – and we all need more of
that! The one who is not a Christian at the time of prayer,

but who has a need and wants God to meet it, will find that the Spirit is bringing him under conviction so that he realises his need of the Saviour, and in the end is being enabled to respond so that he is born again.

This is why one can have confidence in reacting to the problem by affirming the answer, because irrespective of what will happen on that level, the Holy Spirit and the Lord Jesus will cover every need in this life and in the life to come.

This is what I want to say more than anything else: the reason for my involvement in the kind of ministry that I am describing is not because of healing and the other practical help that God gives (though I am vastly appreciative of that); it is because, in a unique way, so far as my experience goes, I have found that it is a wonderful way of showing Christ to people.

So often what the church is saying is of no interest to the general public, which is why the church is largely ignored. But when people know that God is concerned to help them in a tangible way in their real-life situation, it is good news; and when this happens in point of fact, it is a natural and wonderful way to introduce him who is The Good News.

Let no one say that this is an unworthy approach, because it is the approach that Jesus himself made. And it is the approach that we can make today – in his name and for his sake.

"Set your mind to understand"

I share with you a verse of scripture that was a guiding light to me at an earlier time. It is Daniel 10:12. "Daniel, from the first day that you set your mind to understand and humbled yourself before your God, your words have been heard, and I have come because of your words." The fuller passage can be read with profit. "Setting our minds to understand" is all we can do when we need the guidance of the Holy Spirit, and that is what we must do when we need to have more blessing from God than so far we have drawn on. We are wanting God to take us further forward in our vision of what he provides and our experience of what he gives. Not everyone is willing to do this, and we will talk about the reasons for that later on; but for those who are *willing* to be made willing, there is a rich land waiting to be possessed.

What signals are you giving out?

Enough has been said to bring our real selves to the surface. I am not referring to our outward form; that can be good enough. The real question is: what are we affirming underneath and inside?

It is our own peace of mind that is important. It is whether we have problems or answers that is important. And if we are ministers, it is whether our people are being changed by the gospel or not that is important.

May I put several questions that will assist you to make an assessment of your position?

Are you answer-centred or problem-centred?

What are you affirming in the different stress situations in your life?

Do you keep other people in their bondage?

Are the insights in this chapter, i.e. our problems are to bring us to faith in the promises of God, new to you?

If you are familiar with them, do you live by them?

What questions or comments do you have?

If you need to go further, are you willing to be made willing?

A prayer
You might like to use the following prayer:

Father in heaven, I come to you just as I am with all the hurts and bruises of life and ask that you will speak to me and show me the way forward. There are many things that I do not know, but there is one thing that I am sure about and that is: I am in great need. On the outside I do my best to present well, but on the inside … you know me deep down and all the way through and I need you, I need you …

Bless me now as I set my heart to understand and to chasten myself before the Lord my God. As I continue to read these pages I believe you will come to me because of these words and I thank you by faith that you will do this. I pray this in Jesus' name.

2

WHAT YOU NEED DO

1. Praying for yourself

WE HAVE SEEN in Chapter 1 that the problems of man are to bring us to the promises of God; and that these promises are drawn on by faith. There is more to say about faith, but, in any case, it is also the short answer. The longer and more comprehensive answer is what this chapter is all about.

It is in two sections. The first is to do with the thinking and praying that is the special concern of the one who is in need. And in the second part we will look at what can and should be done in the company of others and the great help they can be to us. But first, our own response.

You have to want to get well

I had been asked to see Mrs McPherson because she was unwell, and because her son thought that I might be able to help with the healing ministry. My conversation with her had been "heavy going", and when the opportunity presented itself to speak to her daughter-in-law, I asked her for any comment she would like to make; and this is what she said:

"I don't really think that Mother wants to be any different from what she is now," Jane said. "In a sense, she's never had it so good. People are always asking how she is and fussing over her. She is waited on a good deal and not much is expected of her. In fairness to her, she was spoilt by her husband until his death. The illness she had last year has allowed her to keep things going in the way she got used to. She gives lip service to wanting to get well again but, perhaps without realising it, she is quite content with things as they are."

It isn't always that the person doesn't want to get well. Sometimes he does, but he has become so used to functioning on a less demanding level that he finds the prospect of taking normal adult responsibilities threatening and a problem in itself. I remember Joe Natoli, who had been a depressive for many years. He really wanted to recover and be responsible for his wife and his family again, but this, he told me, was part of his difficulty. It was a real struggle, and although he came out on top in the long run, he had many ups and downs, and his wife and family had to be very patient as they helped him work it all through.

Then there are those who are into drugs – or anything which has a satisfaction to it. It doesn't have to be sinister; smoking is in this category, as are many other things that affect us all. There may be reasons why people want to break the habit, but there are also reasons why they don't. They are in conflict because they want the best of both worlds; to move in one direction creates a bigger pull in the other. They lack the single-minded motivation to come fully into a new life where old things have passed away.

There are many variations on this theme, but they all amount to the same thing: the troubled person must sincerely and consistently *want* to be helped. Jesus made this clear in his ministry to the crippled man at the pool called Bethzatha. The first thing he said to the man was, "Do you want to be healed?"[1] It can be put like this: the more the person concerned wants to be helped, the easier it is to help him; the less he wants help, the more difficult it is to have an effective relationship with him.

Affirm the answer, not the problem

Having said this, it is important not to react to someone with difficulties in this area by *affirming* his or her problem. That will only keep him in his bondage and prevent any progress being made. There is no reason why we cannot believe for him in every way that is needed (see Mark 2:5,11); indeed, his lack of response is all the more reason why we should. In doing this there are several things to keep in mind.

To believe for someone in this position requires a strong and positive identification with him: not with his difficulties, but so that there is a feeling of oneness with him as a person. We have to love him and believe for him, because that is how anyone is helped to draw on God's blessing when he is unable to draw on it for himself. We won't get far just by telling him what to do.

Any impatience or resentment on our part will bring to naught the good we would otherwise do. It isn't easy to avoid this when he is being selfish and causing problems for himself and others. When one fails in this, it is important not to justify the failure by blaming the sick person, because whenever that happens, understandable though it is, no progress is made. But if one admits one has failed and seeks to profit from the admission, there can be an improved performance the next time.

There is something else. A sick person is frequently a manipulator. This means that he tries to use the helping hand to "feather his own nest". When this happens, there is only one thing to do: within the acceptance that has been shown, to face him with what he is doing and tell him plainly it is "not on". Manipulation will continue as long as we let it. If it does not cease, withdraw completely because one cannot win.

Perhaps the most important point to make is that, however small is the person's desire to get well, it is good enough to begin with. He only needs faith like a grain of mustard seed to start things off. I have often been encouraged in my own life by the words, "He will not

break a bruised reed or quench a smouldering wick".[2]
Given time and growth much can be done, provided it is
understood that the person concerned is the one who
makes the final decision.

*A prayer for someone who is not sure that he wants to get
well:*

Father in heaven, you know that I have become used to
being sick and somewhat sorry for myself and that I cannot
face the real world around me all at once. Show me the first
step I have to take and give me the motivation to keep
trying. Bless those around me that they will have the right
balance between accepting me and making me go it alone.
Most of all, enable me to face the truth and to be truthful,
through Christ our Lord.

Don't bury your hurts

Joyce Hansen had ulcerative colitis, which is a distressing
abdominal condition, and it had not responded to medical
treatment or the prayer of faith. She explained that she had
had this trouble for eight years, and when I asked whether
something had happened at that time which might have
been a contributing cause, she replied that there was
nothing. I then asked if there had been any significant
event in her life at that earlier time which she could recall.

"Well, the only thing I can remember during that year is
that one of my children was born."

"Did that make any problems for you?" I asked.

"No ... well, there was only one thing ... I wanted my
sister-in-law to look after our older child, but she didn't
want to do it and made excuses. I made other arrangements, but during the time I was in hospital, the child had
a serious accident, and, rightly or wrongly, I have always
blamed my sister-in-law for what happened. I really think

that if she had looked after Kristine, the accident wouldn't have occurred."

"Does this mean you haven't forgiven your sister-in-law?"

"I'm not sure what to say about that; we have to get on together, and I make it my business to be as pleasant as I can."

"But what are your feelings like deep down – what do you really think about her?"

"Deep down, I am still very resentful and hurt."

I suggested to her that her deep and continuing resentment might have been a causative factor in her physical condition. Then I helped her to draw on the grace of God to forgive her sister-in-law. Joyce was responsive, because she was in the position where *she had to do something about it* if there was to be any change for the better. She didn't get it right all at once, but she persevered until she was able to say, "I can really go forward to Mavis now with no reservation or hurt."

When this had been thoroughly worked through, the colitis cleared up and has not returned.

Medical research

In case there is any uncertainty about the consequence of buried hurts, let us look at what three medical authorities have to say. First, Professor Hans Selye, who has been the leading medical researcher on stress in the United States for many years and is the author of several books on this subject: "Innumerable studies of disease processes have shown that stress, more than any other factor, determines whether there is a proper balance in our lives. Most of us are born healthy, but if the harmful stresses resulting from improper perception, personal misbehaviour and environmental conditions tip the balance, we slide down the slope from health to disease. There can be no doubt that stress diseases are on the increase."[3]

And now Dr Carl Simonton, Director of the Cancer

Counselling and Research Centre in Fort Worth: "We believe that cancer is often an indication of problems elsewhere in an individual's life. Problems aggravated and compounded by a series of stresses, six to eighteen months prior to the onset of cancer. The cancer patient has typically responded to these problems and stresses with a deep sense of hopelessness or 'giving-up'. This emotional response, we believe, in turn triggers a set of physiological responses that suppress the body's natural defences and make it susceptible to producing abnormal cells."[4]

Finally, Dr Wolf and Dr Goodell, whom Professor Selye quotes with approval: "The goal of medicine should be to understand the patient as a person: establish the circumstances that precipitated his illness – the underlying conflicts, hostilities, and griefs; in short, the bruised nature of his emotional state. The physician needs to know as much about emotions and emotional maladjustments as about disease symptoms and drugs. This approach holds more promise of cure than anything medicine has given man."[5]

What can we do?

Just as we can react at a later time by affirming the answer and not the problem, so too we can react in a way that changes the bad into good when the stress *first presents itself* at our doorstep. It is exactly for this kind of situation that our Lord Jesus Christ gave the teaching, "Love your enemies, do good to those who hate you, bless those who curse you, pray for those who abuse you. To him who strikes you on the cheek, offer him the other also . . . "[6] And if forgiveness is involved, "Leave your gift there before the altar and go; first be reconciled to your brother, and then come and offer your gift."[7] St Paul says, "Give thanks in all circumstances; for this is the will of God in Christ Jesus for you."[8]

This means that we do not take the stress into ourselves. Instead, we draw on the positive and creative things that come from Jesus. In so far as it is a burden, we cast our burden upon the Lord – and leave it there. He gives us his strength in return, relevant to our circumstances. And to the degree that this is faithfully followed through, it may well be that those who have caused the hurt will be brought to contrition by our Christian witness.

It may be very important to share any distress we have felt with a trusted friend, and as close to the time of the incident as possible. With matters that concern us personally, we often cannot "see the wood for the trees". Our emotions have become involved, and, in some degree, hurt and resentment may have taken root, even when we have tried to respond as we should. Happy is the person who has someone to whom he can open his heart, someone who will listen and understand and sift the wheat from the tares. There is a comfort that comes from a problem shared, and there is a blessing of God that comes when others pray.

But what about the hurt that has been buried? What can we do about that? Again, the person must want to be helped. All too frequently there is an unwillingness to forgive and forget. Or it may be that the problem has been affirmed for so long, and imagination has added so much to fact, that the mountain is a mountain indeed.

The ministry needed in this case is that of "inner healing". Buried hurts, whether they are remembered or forgotten, are still in the tissue of the mind, and very much affect our life in the present. They have built up over the years, one hurt leading to another, until we have become the complex characters we are today. In my own counselling practice, I spend a lot of time just helping the person concerned to understand himself. This is always worthwhile and, as often as not, is something of a revelation to him. It means being concerned to find the hurts that have combined to produce the problem. The story I have just told of Joyce Hansen is a typical illustration.

Very likely the person concerned has to do something himself. If there has been an open break in relationships, steps have to be taken to make things right – a letter written, an apology made, forgiveness offered as well as sought. But if the other person knows nothing about the felt difficulty, it may only make for embarrassment to bring it up. In that case (and almost always), it is enough for the one who has the difficulty to take appropriate steps to draw on healing himself, and not to canvass it any further.

There will need to be prayer for the healing of those memories, whereby we affirm that God is coming into the past so that "the old has passed away".[9] This kind of believing prayer has to be made in depth, and because of that, probably in a continuing way. It stands to reason that old hurts are not going to be easy to root out, and solving one problem often reveals another. Someone else's faith may well need to be added to that of the person concerned – and again in an on-going way.

Inner healing and Holy Communion

However needful and valuable the prayer help of others, it is unwise to rely on that too much. It can be a substitute for developing one's own prayer capacity. Here is a helpful suggestion for someone who needs inner healing and at the same time wants to grow in his own faith.

Plan on going to Holy Communion each week with a special intention. Bring to mind all the matters in the last year for which you need healing. Work through them in prayer, make restitution where necessary, and believe that in receiving the sacrament you are drawing on healing for those hurts. Consciously believe this is what God is doing and affirm it by faith. Next week do the same for the year previous to that, and so on. The further you go back, the less you will remember, but don't be put off by that; God knows every need you have, and, in any case, you are believing for the healing of the past whether it is remembered or not.

I have a friend who did this in a meaningful way and drew on the promise of Psalm 23, "He restores my soul". It had an amusing consequence we did not anticipate; his peace of mind was such that he put on a good deal of weight! He blamed me for this, and I could only reply, "You can't win all the time!"

Inner healing and the fullness of the Holy Spirit

I would like to talk about this now from a very different perspective. When Agnes Sanford came to Sydney at Easter, 1961, she conducted a great teaching mission on the healing ministry in St Andrew's Cathedral, which overflowed with people night after night. The healing ministry in the Cathedral had begun in the previous year, and after the honeymoon period was over, I soon found that more of the power of the Holy Spirit was needed for this ministry than, at the time, I possessed. My theological approach at that time did not approve of a "second blessing", but need finally outweighed argument, and I approached Mrs Sanford and asked if she could assist me.

She invited me to come to her hotel, and after a short preliminary conversation, she stood behind me, rested her hands lightly on my head, and began to pray. And she prayed the prayer of faith that I be filled with the Spirit. Nothing whatever happened, except that I had an overwhelming feeling it was like praying for the wall! After five minutes or so of this, Mrs Sanford suddenly stopped, and in her kindly but plain way said, "This is getting nowhere!" Well, we agreed on that!

Then she began to pray again, this time just letting the Holy Spirit guide her prayer as needed. After a time, she began to refer to things that had happened in my early life – things that no one knew about apart from me. These were times when I had reacted to stress by being emotionally hurt, and, because I knew no differently, the hurt had been buried. She went from one experience to another, about four or five in all, and she spoke of them almost as if she had been there. I wasn't embarrassed so much as incredulous to hear someone whom I hardly knew praying in this fashion. It was my introduction to the "gift of knowledge", whereby the Holy Spirit allows a person to know something that is necessary for his ministry to be effective.

When Mrs Sanford had finished praying, she explained to me that, when we are hurt, the defence mechanisms we erect around ourselves for protection keep out not only harm, but also the deeper blessings of God. I knew the first point, but certainly not the second.

At her suggestion we met again a couple of days later, this time at the Cathedral, and she prayed for me again. On this occasion it was for the healing of those past hurts. The first prayer had been diagnostic; the second was remedial. Again it was a prayer in depth (it lasted about twenty minutes), and I felt a strange calm as a result.

Afterwards, as I was going through the Cathedral to our Chapter House to check on a morning meeting Mrs Sanford was going to address, a very strange experience came to me. Let me explain that I am really a very down-to-earth person – not given at all to visions or flights of fancy. But as I walked across the Cathedral, there appeared in front of me something like an upturned cup, though not, it seemed, made of any earthly material. As I looked at it, it cracked right across the middle from side to side like a broken knee-cap. At the time I had no idea what it meant, but later something of the meaning came to me – I believe it represented my defence mechanisms and that they had been broken by the power of the Holy Spirit.

On the evening before Agnes returned to the United States, I had a meal with her and the Reverend David Williams, who had also been involved in her visit. David was on the staff of Christ Church St Laurence, one of our Anglican parishes in Sydney, and he suggested that we call into his church to pray before we finally took Agnes back to her hotel. We took turns to pray for one another, and they kindly prayed for me first. This time Agnes prayed that I be filled with the Spirit, and, almost before she opened her mouth, I was overwhelmed with God's blessing. I felt I was being immersed – saturated – in the

Holy Spirit so that he went all the way through me. By comparison, I could not help feeling that my experience of the Spirit in conversion had been "on the surface" only. What happened changed my life and ministry in a wonderful way, and gave me an awareness of the person and ministry of the Holy Spirit which I did not have before, and which I have always had since.

I could say much more of what this has meant to me, but that is not quite the point of the illustration. My reason for relating it is to show that buried hurts lead to defence mechanisms, and defence mechanisms not only help to keep out further hurt, but can keep out the deeper experiences of the Holy Spirit. As far as I was concerned, it was only when there had been a meaningful healing of those hurts and their defences that I was able to draw on the fuller experience that God had for me.

Don't bury your hurts – and hurts that have been buried need to be healed.

A prayer for someone with buried hurts

Loving Father, you are the only one to whom I can open my inner feelings. It is so difficult to think of my emotional life being any different from what it has been. At least I begin to open myself to you and ask that you will come in and heal me deep down. Thank you by faith that you are doing that now. O, the relief to feel the ointment of your love on my hurts and griefs. Continue to do this, I pray, and make me complete, lacking in nothing, because of Jesus.

Repent

To repent means that we turn from whatever hinders our relationship with God. Repentance was one of the great essentials in the ministry of Jesus, and it is equally relevant to us today. And, sadly, it is a much neglected emphasis.

The Mary Sisters

The great modern exponents of repentance are the evangelical Sisterhood of Mary, who have their mother house at Darmstadt in West Germany and smaller houses in many parts of the world. The circumstances of their formation in 1947 give the clue to their understanding and practice of repentance. During World War II, their city of Darmstadt had been razed to the ground by Allied bombing. Seeing this as God's judgment, they repented of their personal sins and the sins of their nation during the war. Out of this movement of repentance, and love for Jesus, the sisterhood was born.

They have continued to make repentance the keynote of their own walk with God and their ministry with others. In principle, and as I understand it, their insight and affirmation is that God has provided his kingdom for us, and the only thing that prevents the believer from having the kingdom blessing is unrepented sin. If we do not have the blessing we need, God in effect is saying that there is something wrong in our relationship with him and with each other, and that we need to turn from that sin, so that we can have a restoration of the kingdom blessing. Repentance is therefore not negative, but rather something to be welcomed in a positive way, that we may have the blessing God has provided.

A charming story told by Mother Basilea in her book *Realities* makes the point. Not long after the sisterhood had been formed and they were building their chapel by themselves, they ran into trouble. There was a small rail track that led to the building site, and on it ran a dump-cart, used to wheel the excavated earth out of the way. At one stage the dump-cart kept jumping the rails, and no amount of adjustment made any difference.

Finally, the Mary Sisters who were working on the chapel went to their prayer tent nearby and began to pray. One of the sisters then confessed that she had a grudge against one of the other sisters, and asked to be forgiven. Then another sister admitted her faults in relationships, and sought to make amends. It wasn't long before there was a heartfelt change of attitude in those relationships about which they had been convicted. And Mother Basilea solemnly records that the dump-cart never jumped the rails again![10]

The principle in the story is the important thing, as it applies to our daily lives. Repentance is not something for Ash Wednesday only; it is for every moment and every day of the week. Rightly understood, repentance is essentially positive, and enables us to draw on the promised blessing of God in a way that we may know little about if it is neglected. For good reason, Mother Basilea of the Mary Sisters called her best-known book, *Repentance, the Joy-filled Life*.

If you need to find healing, you may well need to find repentance also.

A prayer for repentance

Lord and judge, I turn away from my sin and all that hinders my relationship with you. I would make a completely new start with you and with others. Thank you that this can be done and you are enabling me to do it. If I should fail and return to my sin, lift me up again by the ministry of the Holy Spirit. By faith I affirm that I am completely turned to you and that your joy is filling me now. Glory be to Jesus.

Believe

When our Lord summed up what we should do to draw on blessing from God, he majored on faith, "According to your faith be it done to you".[11] To the father of a sick boy he said, "All things are possible to him who believes."[12] Conversely, to the disciples who had failed to heal, he said that it was "because of your little faith".[13] With the ministry of the apostles, Paul, for example, saw that the cripple "had faith to be made well".[14] As far as healing today is concerned, we have the plain statement in James

5, that the prayer offered in faith will make the sick person well. One of the broad themes in the New Testament is faith. More than that, the writer to the Hebrews states that "without faith it is impossible to please God".

It is therefore of the utmost importance that we know this, and that we know what has been revealed about faith itself – the more so because there is great confusion and misunderstanding in Christian circles about this vital matter. We have already said there is a lack of vision that the promises of God reveal the will of God. As a consequence, there is no real concern to understand faith as it is described in the Bible, that we might draw on those promises in real life. And even where faith is exercised effectively, as in conversion, there is little or no understanding about the scriptural basis of what we are doing.

Yet if we look at this example it may enable us to sort the matter out and come to guidelines that are theologically sound and pastorally effective.

Faith for conversion ...

When we think about conversion, we begin with the promise that if we believe on Christ we will be saved. We then use (in evangelical circles) certain expressions that are designed to help the seeker draw on the blessing of Christ and come into the reality of being born again. We speak about "accepting the Lord Jesus Christ as our own personal Saviour" and "making a decision for Christ". It will come as a shock to many to be told that neither of these hallowed expressions is to be found in scripture, or anything like them!

What *is* found in scripture about drawing on blessing from God is in Mark 11, where Jesus said, "Whatever you ask in prayer, believe that you have received it, and it will be yours", and just previously he had said in the same connection "and does not doubt in his heart". The value of the colloquial expression about "accepting Christ" is that it puts into language which can be easily understood the instruction given by scripture, i.e. we must believe that we "have received" him. Likewise, the value of "making a decision" is that it enables us to believe so that we do "not doubt in (our) heart".

I am not deprecating the use of these expressions, provided that we understand why they are effective and where their authority comes from. Granted this, I would advocate their use on *all* occasions where faith is being exercised for the promises of God. Because once we know the principle of faith whereby we appropriate the promise of new life in Christ, we have the principle that applies with all the other promises of God. All the promises are promises, and the means by which we appropriate them is always faith; and faith is the same – irrespective of what promise is being drawn on. If any confirmation of this fact is needed, it can be found in James 5, verses 14 and 15, "The prayer of faith will save the sick man, and the Lord will raise him up, and if he has committed sins, he will be forgiven." It is the same prayer of faith that saves, heals and forgives.*

There is more to be clear about. When as a young man I accepted Christ and made a decision for him, I found no change whatsoever in my life. When I subsequently told my rector, the Reverend (now Canon) Rudolph Dillon, he was quick to point out that theological faith is not what we see but what we hope for; and this means that we are to believe for the blessing before we have it in point of fact. At first I found this confusing and said I did not *feel* any different. His reply was that we do not affirm it with our

---

*This is not to say that to draw on the promise of healing *is the same* as to draw on the promise of salvation; because, while salvation is always available in this life, there are limitations to healing as age increases and strength declines. What we have said is that healing and salvation (and all the promises of God) are drawn on *in the same way*, i.e. by faith which believes that you have received these things so that you do not doubt in your heart. As to the limitations of healing, we discuss that later in our story.

feelings, but with our mind. Dr John Stott rightly points out that "your mind matters". I can remember how I disciplined my thinking so that this was done. Even so, nothing happened at once and nothing ever came out of the blue, so to speak. But as I continued to affirm the promise by faith and believed in what I hoped for, gradually there came a witness of the Spirit that Christ was in my life and that I was at one with the Father.

Let us put these insights together. By belief or faith we mean, to use colloquial language, that we "accept" the promise and "make a decision" to that end; or as scripture puts it, we believe we receive it so that we do not doubt in our heart. Further to this, faith means that we affirm this with our mind before we have the blessing in reality. Or, to use the words of scripture, "Faith is the assurance of things hoped for, the conviction of things not seen."[15]

It follows that when we react to permitted difficulties by having faith for the relevant promise of God, it means we accept the promise by making a decision to that effect and continue to affirm it with our mind until it is what we have in fact. Our part is to accept, decide and affirm.

... and faith for healing

Let us say that someone has the 'flu and has taken to his bed. If that is what he accepts, then the sickness will run its usual course. But if he knows there is a provision of healing, and he accepts and affirms it so that that is what he is drawing on, the sickness is thereby being shortened. If, better still, he puts his faith into action and gets up and goes about his business, reacting to any symptoms by affirming healing in his mind by faith, he will get better more quickly still. As with everything, balance and common sense are necessary. One would not react to a heart attack in that way. If there is any uncertainty as to what can be done, or not done, one's doctor should be consulted.

Back to the 'flu. If, on a subsequent occasion he feels 'flu symptoms coming on, and rebukes them and affirms

wholeness and holds on to that, there is more than an even
chance that he will not go down with sickness. If he
continues to act like this, it won't be long before the 'flu
does not come near him at all. Try it – you have nothing to
lose except the 'flu! And you will be started in the healing
ministry.

Apply this now in a more general area. Consider, for
example, the problem of loneliness. This is the most
common social need and, indeed, there are areas of
loneliness in the life of everyone. If we affirm our
loneliness, it will only continue and worsen; but if we
react to it by knowing that Christ has said, "I am with you
always", [16] and ". . . if anyone hears my voice and opens the
door, I will come in to him and eat with him, and he with
me",[17] we can then draw on this provision by accepting it
and affirming it in an ongoing way. If our circumstances
are not changed straight away, we discipline our mind to
believe it before we have it in reality. When that is done, we
will find, if not all at once, then progressively, that we
have the Divine Friend in our life in every way that is
needful to us.

If it is human friendship we want (and we all need that),
it is to be believed for in exactly the same way. One of the
earliest things God said is that it is not good for man to be
alone. This shows clearly that our heavenly Father is
concerned to meet everyone's needs on the level of human
relationships. To those who are called to Christian
marriage, it is right and good for them to believe for a God-
given partner. We have all seen beautiful things happen in
that way because of faith.

Prayer in the present tense
If you are like me, you may well have trouble in
changing over from accepting the problem to accepting
the answer. I have found that the tug of the difficulty can
be so great that, despite my endeavour to accept the
provision God has made, I come to the point where I just
can't continue to try and affirm the answer any longer and,

instead, go back to affirming things as they are. But I also find that when I apply myself to this at a later time it can be done more effectively, even though I may come to a stopping place again because the problem is so deeply entrenched within me. But I can also say that when I have persevered, I have come ultimately to an acceptance and affirmation of the answer by faith that increasingly transforms the circumstances, whether they be my own or those of someone else.*

We will be helped to do this by believing that our prayer is being answered in a present-tense kind of way. Actually, the real requirement, Jesus said, is to believe that we "have received" the answer to our prayer (see Mark 11:24 R.S.V.). This is a faith statement, i.e. we are affirming something before we have it in point of fact. But if that is too difficult, I encourage people who are exercising faith to affirm, "Thank you Father, you are healing me now."

When Norman Vincent Peale spoke at the healing service in St Andrew's Cathedral, he made this point himself and suggested that it be visualised as well. In one of his graphic illustrations, he told of a man who had been advised by his doctor that medical tests indicated he was heading for serious physical breakdown. After the man left the doctor's rooms, he was suddenly struck by God's wonderful creation around him, and was reminded of the blessing of wholeness that was available to him because of Christ. He consciously breathed in, and at the same time affirmed that he was drawing on the wholeness and healing of God for his need. He did this in a continuing way, the act of breathing in being an outward and visible

---

*There are those who raise a theological difficulty about *persevering* in prayer when it comes to healing. But if there is nothing wrong (and no one suggests there is), in persevering in faith for conversion and other provisions of God, why is it made out to be a problem with healing? One can only suggest that those who have this difficulty work through the insights that have been given and be consistent in their approach.

sign of what he was doing in an inward and invisible way. After some months of this he returned to his physician, who ran another series of tests and found that the potential trouble had disappeared.

We need to be open to growth and development in these things. God does not stand still, and neither should we. One of the most satisfying aspects of praying in the Spirit is to find this happening as our heavenly Father is enabled to "take over" in our lives more and more. As the reality of the promises of God and the prayer of faith become more deeply ingrained within us, we will find our mind starting to "tick over" in a positive and believing way with little conscious effort on our part.

Those who have read my earlier book will remember the story of the hunchback boy who was healed. The people mainly responsible for exercising faith on his behalf, until he was old enough to be involved himself, were his parents. Sometimes his mother would contact me on the phone about something or other, and after the conversation was over I would always feel very uplifted by the Spirit of God. This was because her mind was automatically "ticking over" in believing for the blessing of God, and although we may not have been talking about spiritual matters, this came my way because of our conversation.

To summarise: we have said that we are to apply our "conversion" understanding of faith to each and all the promises of God; we are to believe that our prayer is being answered in a present-tense way; and that we can assist our inward conviction by giving it an outward form.

It may help us to see this more clearly if we realise that, almost certainly, this is being done already – but in terms of the sickness or whatever else is the problem situation. That is, we have accepted the difficulty and we are affirming it in a continuing way, both inwardly and outwardly.

But, of course, our thesis is that instead of affirming what comes from the sin of the world and is seen, we are to affirm what comes from the kingdom of God and is believed *before* it is seen. Then our belief will not perpetuate our problem but will move our mountain.

A prayer of belief

O God of heaven and earth, I praise you that you have drawn close to us in Christ and that we can draw close to you through faith. Thank you for the many gracious promises you have made. I now respond and put my faith into action and believe that as your provisions are being received, so your kingdom is being extended in me and in others, through the working of the Holy Spirit. Thank you, Father, you are healing me now.

Obey

There is something more we have to do to have God's promised blessings. Jesus said, "Not everyone who says to me, 'Lord, Lord,' shall enter the kingdom of heaven, but he who does the will of my Father who is in heaven."[18]

To do the will of the Father means that we obey him. Not that we are made right with the Father because we obey; we are made right because of what Jesus has done on the cross on our behalf. Our obedience is the badge or sign whereby we show God and other people that our faith for salvation is sincere and lasting. We are not saved by obedience, but we are not saved without it.

James said that doing the will of God – being obedient – means we are to "visit orphans and widows in their affliction, and to keep oneself unstained from the world."[19] Obedience is both good works and personal holiness. It is the fruit of our Christian walk that we offer God in the day when we render an account of our stewardship. Obedience is more than this, but it includes this.

While it does not contribute to our salvation, it does have eternal significance. This was what Jesus was referring to when he spoke of some being given authority

over ten cities and others over five, and of some who lost
everything.[20] There is a judgment for the Christian, and it
will be on the matter of his obedience. Would that this was
more emphasised in our church teaching!

I am hesitant to add this, but as I believe it, I will. If a
"come to Jesus" ministry is not firmly set in the context
that we have also to repent and obey, I have the utmost
reservation about the validity of that ministry. No one
values the evangelical approach more than I do; I owe my
conversion to it, and would that it were extended! But the
test of our relationship with Christ is not only in what we
say; it is also in what we do and what we are. There is no
such thing as "cheap grace".

Only God can make the assessment as to whether we
have obeyed as well as believed. But when our turn comes
to stand before the Judge "to whom all hearts are open, all
desires known, and from whom no secrets are hidden",[21]
that will be the question he will address to the Christian.

We are to react to our permitted difficulties by coming to
faith in the promises of God, which means we are to repent
and believe – and obey.

A prayer of obedience

Lord and king, prepare me to take responsibilities in
your kingdom on earth and in your kingdom in heaven.
Give me, by your grace, that reality of holiness and service
that is pleasing to you. Increase my vision of these things
and the response I need to make, that Christ, who was
obedient unto death, may be glorified.

Forgive and forget

Some reference has already been made to this matter, but as
it is so important and is specifically referred to by Jesus on
a number of occasions, we will develop it further. It can be
put like this: if you are believing for healing or for any of
the promises of God and you find that things are not
working out in the way they need to, then think of what
Jesus said, "... whenever you stand praying, forgive, if

you have anything against anyone". The importance of this is readily seen when the next words are also brought to mind, ". . . so that your Father may forgive you your trespasses. But if you do not forgive, neither will your Father forgive your trespasses."[22]

This passage immediately follows the great teaching on faith that we have just referred to. If we are wanting to exercise faith, we have to be concerned, at the same time, with our forgiveness of others, because if we do not forgive, neither will our heavenly Father forgive us. One doesn't have to be a theologian to see that, if we are in a state of being unforgiven by God, we are not going to get far in our prayers. It is obvious that praying and forgiving are linked together in a way that cannot be ignored. If we are going to pray in faith effectively, we have to forgive meaningfully.

Personal forgiveness

We all know how difficult this can be. Which of us does not burn with righteous indignation over some hurt from those who should know better, including some who profess and call themselves Christians? And how easy it is to keep the memory alive by reliving it again to justify one's position. But understandable as it is, we are only making a rod for our own back. Apart from keeping others in their bondage, we are seriously limiting the effectiveness of our prayer life.

The clue to being able to forgive is in the words, "if you have anything against anyone". For many years I thought this standard of complete forgiveness was so impossible to achieve that I did not take it seriously. Now I realise that this was because I had the "forgive but can't forget" approach. Given that, it wasn't long before one was affirming unforgiveness again – and back to "square one".

When at last I forgave everything and everyone, so that I did forget, I found to my surprise and joy that it was not only possible but easy, and it worked perfectly. You see, when we do it so that there is nothing left to do, there is nothing left to cause further trouble and bring back memories. The slate is wiped completely clean, and we make a new and fresh start.

This is so important, and so easy when we follow through the instructions. Here is a prayer that you may like to use straight away: "Thank you, Father, that though my sins are as scarlet you make them whiter than snow through the blood of Jesus. I now forgive all others in the same way as you have forgiven me, and affirm, by faith, that I now make a completely new start in my relationships, as I pray that others will make a new start with me, for Jesus' sake."

One of my colleagues, the Reverend John Squires, says that "the past is Satan's territory". He means that Satan uses our past to accuse us in our present. That is so true. But John goes on to say that when we have fully forgiven others and have been fully forgiven by God, Satan has nothing of which to accuse us – then the past is God's territory.

If my years in the healing ministry have taught me one thing more than another, it is that nothing contributes more to sickness than resentment, and more to healing than to forgive and forget.

*   *   *

This has been the personal side of drawing on divine healing. It is appreciated, of course, that the more seriously ill the person is, the less he will be able to apply himself to these matters. But that doesn't lessen the need to explain what is involved. Certainly it needs to be said that the more the sick person and his family *understand* the healing ministry and can act intelligently in drawing on the promised blessing, the more easily and effectively will the answer to prayer be experienced.

Probably it is a good idea to make a pause here in reading, and treat what has been written in the first section as being a chapter in itself. There is a good deal to reflect on. Then when you are ready, continue with the next section which is much shorter.

2. Praying with others

Now we come to that aspect of healing that is drawn on
with others. If we have faith to "call for the elders of the
church", it is then their responsibility to believe with us
and for us. This section will explain what that means and
how we can share in it.

Our way of presenting the following material is
somewhat different from our exposition so far. We are
going to describe in some detail the healing ministry as it
is practised in St Andrew's Cathedral, Sydney. As well as
being of interest, it will set out the corporate side of the
ministry as we see it. This is not to say that others are to
copy what we do; they must follow God's leading as to
what is appropriate in their setting. The important thing
is to understand the principles that are involved, put them
into operation and partake of them.

Join a healing congregation
This is something that everyone who is seeking healing
ought to do. Join and stay. The only thing that really
worries me is the person in need who comes to the healing
service once or twice and is not seen again. Experience has
shown that it is those who "go it alone" who can end up
being hurt and disillusioned with what happens. It only
stands to reason. We all need support, we all need faith
from the outside, we all need the right ministry at the right
time. Granted that, experience again shows that God
meets every need, irrespective of what happens on the level
of healing.

I can hear people saying, "Well, where is there a healing
service in my church that I can attend?" A good question –
and a good reason why the main-line churches should be
concerned to provide this ministry within their structure.
Then their membership and others can come to Mother
Church as they want to and as they need to.

The healing service at St Andrew's Cathedral

As we describe our healing service and congregational life, it will have the effect of setting out something of our growth in insight and activity, and the factors that we see to be important in drawing on healing and wholeness from God. It may not be irrelevant to note that our ministry is said to be the largest of its kind in the world – after that of Paul Yonggi Cho in Seoul, Korea.

Our service is intended to be a presentation of the healing ministry as it is set out in James 5:14,15. It is worth having these words in our mind as we begin, "Is any among you sick? Let him call for the elders of the church, and let them pray over him, anointing him with oil in the name of the Lord; and the prayer of faith will save the sick man, and the Lord will raise him up; and if he has committed sins, he will be forgiven."

First days

When I entered into the conviction that Jesus heals today because he is the same now as in the days of his earthly ministry, we began to hold a regular healing service straight away. Often people only *talk* about healing, or it is something that their minister does on his own; or if a service is held, it is too infrequent to be effective. I can only say that the weekly service of divine healing has always been the central point of our activity, and that it is the source of what strength, blessing and outreach we have drawn on.

The first healing service was held in St Andrew's Cathedral on the last Wednesday in September 1960. There was never a minister who knew less about what he was setting out to do, but I had something that was priceless: a conviction given, I believe, by the Holy Spirit.

After we had been meeting for a couple of weeks, a woman came forward saying that she had a serious infection in her middle ear which had not so far responded to medical treatment, and that her doctor had expressed concern about her condition. Hardly knowing what to do,

I placed my hands upon her head and said the prayer of faith in a faltering and tentative way. She came back the next day and said she had been healed. And so we began.

Sometimes I wish we could recall the honeymoon period. We were child-like in that we believed so that we did not doubt in our heart. We laid hands on people and they recovered, usually at once, including those with cancer. It seemed to be straight out of the New Testament. Our numbers quickly grew, so that we had to move out of the chapel into the main body of the Cathedral.

Wonderful as the honeymoon period was, it did not last, and within a few months we began striving in prayer rather than resting in faith. The blessings tapered off, and answers to prayer tended to come in a progressive way rather than being immediate. This was when I was ministered to by Agnes Sanford and drew on the fullness of the Holy Spirit. Meaningful as this was, it did not return me to the earlier time, though it gave me, and others who also began to draw on this dimension, a much more mature experience of the Holy Spirit, and it set us up in a more enduring way, so that the ministry grew as time went by. That growth has never ceased. Perhaps our main characteristic is that "forgetting what lies behind and straining forward to what lies ahead",[23] we continue to expand.

The present time

I am now going to describe in some detail the healing service as it is at the present time. It is still held on a Wednesday night at 6 o'clock, and you need to be there in good time to get a seat. After twenty-three years, more people attend the service than at any previous time. All through the day a small army of workers have been preparing in different ways: library, bookstall, cassettes, refreshments, banners, prayer requests, sermon notes, service sheets, music, P.A. arrangements, etc. Finally, everything is ready as people start to arrive from mid-afternoon. Between 5.30 and 6.00 p.m. there is often a

queue at the doors waiting to get in. But all who come are
warmly and individually welcomed as they enter and are
shown to a seat. How people are received is most
important; it sets the tone of everything else that will
subsequently happen. So often people say, "It was the way
I was welcomed at the door . . . there was a warmth of love
as soon as I came in."

Once a month we have a shortened service of Holy
Communion at 5.30 p.m. for those who are communi-
cants, several hundred being present. On other nights
there is a praise time before the service, led by our
musicians with piano and organ accompaniment. As well
as the great hymns of the church, we use the music that has
come from the Renewal Movement. It seems to give a
release of the Spirit as it instructs and inspires.

The service itself has a regular format, though it is not
so rigid as to limit spontaneity. Someone has described it
as "a low-key charismatic service". "All things should be
done decently and in order"[24] is one side of the story, and
the other is, "where the Spirit of the Lord is, there is
freedom".[25] The majority of those attending are involved
in the Renewal Movement, but there are also those who are
not. There is absolutely no division on this issue; everyone
is accepted whatever his background and conviction, and
there is a happy and positive relationship of inter-
dependence and mutual respect.

We begin with prayer, hymn singing, and then a
welcome and greeting time. There are always visitors, and
they are asked to identify themselves by raising their hand;
welcomers give them a ribbon which they are asked to
wear, and which will identify them throughout the
evening so that they are properly cared for. The greeting
time is very important and serves a variety of purposes:
meeting old and new friends, exchanging a Christian
greeting, following up someone who was ministered to
last week and, more generally, allowing the Holy Spirit to
be stirred up through the reality of Christian fellowship.
This may last five minutes or more, with everybody

moving around and sharing in the way that is right as far as they are concerned. It is a part of the service that is easy to start and difficult to bring to an end!

This is followed by a testimony, the only requirement being that it must not belong to "the blue remembered hills". There is no shortage of things to say on this level, whether it comes from someone in the congregation, or from our postal congregation (more about this later), or, increasingly, from our radio audience. After this, or at another point in the service, we often invite people to stand who have a testimony to give of God's blessing received during the last week. It does not have to be spectacular, it may be "first the blade",[26] but as long as it is meaningful and what God has done, it is a testimony. More people stand at this point to return thanks for blessings received than stand at any other time to ask for prayer because they are in need. Testimonies are invariably followed by the singing of "Praise God" to the tune "Amazing Grace", which has been the healing service song over all the years.

The broadcast

After a reading of the scriptures, the broadcast segment begins. The next half-hour of the service is recorded by the Christian Broadcasting Association, and is broadcast on Sunday night at 9 o'clock over their Station 2 CBA-FM to an audience of about two hundred and fifty thousand people. Other FM stations also broadcast the service at other times. The broadcast begins with a hymn and is followed by a teaching address, then by a solo and by the first part of the laying on of hands, and it concludes with more singing.

I would like to say more about the broadcast. When the Reverend Vernon Turner, the Founder-Director of CBA, first raised the idea of putting the healing service on air, we had serious reservations – how, for example, could the laying on of hands be communicated by radio? As it has turned out, not only have there been no problems, but Vernon maintains it is the best thing they have recorded and broadcast in twenty-five years! The sounds of people moving around and praying are all picked up on the microphones and give a feeling of activity that makes for reality.

One Wednesday, because of a technical fault, the station was limited to playing records; the tape-recorded programmes could not be used. There were a number of phone enquiries during the day asking where was this programme or that; but when it came to the time when the healing service is broadcast, the phones were jammed with calls: "Where is the healing service?" It is their most popular programme.

The sermon and the sermon notes

The teaching address is considered to be very important, and I usually give a series of three addresses under a general title, such as:

Are you at the crossroads?
(1) Problems can lead to breakdown
(2) Problems can lead to healing
(3) Problems can lead to conversion

The following week one of my colleagues will preach, and then I will begin another series, such as:

My difficulty is ...
(1) Having faith for myself
(2) Loving other people all the time
(3) Concentrating in prayer

In a way which, like Topsy, "just grow'd", the address is printed out in what we call "sermon notes". This was begun through the initiative of Deaconess Gwyneth Hall, who is one of our main workers, and it has become an essential part of our ministry and outreach. In case it is of interest, perhaps I should explain that a typescript of the address is prepared and edited and then printed to fill either side of a foolscap sheet. When people come on the Wednesday night, they pick up the sermon notes for the address given the previous week. One thousand are taken by people who come to the service, and another four thousand are sent out through the post to people who have asked for them. The main areas of distribution are in Australia and New Zealand, but they also go into most countries of the world and have been remarkably used by God over the years. Our experience is that people like to read the sermon they have heard or, if they belong to our postal or radio congregation, to read the teaching address although they cannot attend the service. They also lead to a fruitful correspondence ministry as well as a continuing flow of prayer requests.

The laying on of hands

The laying on of hands is the climax of the service, and enables those in need to be prayed for by members of the congregation. This was at first administered by the clergy and a select group of lay people who were set aside for this work and who exercised a splendid ministry. But the disadvantage of having a ministry that is "out front" is that the rest of the congregation only say "amen". Some years ago we widened this ministry so that anyone could lay on hands provided that:

He was a converted Christian

He was a regular member of the congregation

He believed it was right for him to lay on hands on this occasion – that is, he was at one with the Lord and with his brethren.

It needs to be said that we came to this arrangement because the congregation had reached the point, from both experience gained and instruction given, of being able to exercise these responsibilities in an effective way. They have more than fulfilled what was expected of them, and we would not think of reverting to the former method. People receiving the laying on of hands frequently testify that the help they have received from members of the congregation has been anointed by the Holy Spirit. There is no question about that. It is more than laying on hands. Every member of the congregation is expected to have an active ministry outreach in a way that suits his or her gifts and personality. I cannot begin to say how good it is – gentle, purposeful, loving, skilful, patient, committed, prayerful, effective. God uses them in a remarkable way.

For the actual laying on of hands, we invite people who wish to receive this ministry to raise their hand, and then the members of the congregation gather round in groups of three or four and enquire the need of the person who is seeking ministry. First there is a prayer from the prayer desk and our prayer book; then the members of the group pray and relate their prayer to the need that has been shared with them. It is a moving sight to see up to one hundred groups at prayer in the Cathedral at this time.

The leaders, clerical and lay, are quietly moving about while this is taking place to make sure everything works out as it should. They will assist in forming the groups, join in prayer where necessary, or give a word of guidance and encouragement. But there is one thing our leaders must not do: they must not take over the ministry. They are there to *enable* the ministry to be exercised by the general body of believers. We not only believe in the "ministry of all believers", but we practise it, and it is the mainstay of all that we do.

Perhaps it should be explained that there is nothing magic about the laying on of hands. It is an outward and visible sign of the inward and invisible faith that those praying are sharing with the person being prayed for. It can also be an effectual sign, because people will sometimes testify that the power of God has passed through their hands into the person for whom prayer has been made. The hands should be lightly placed on the head or shoulders, though there is no reason why they cannot be placed on the affected part if that is otherwise appropriate. Not least, touching is a therapeutic thing as well as an act of compassion and support.

After the laying on of hands there usually follows a time of prayer, when the teaching in the address that has been given that night is drawn on, and people are invited to apply it to themselves, so that they stand and corporate prayer is made for them. It is this application of ministry that helps to make the healing service so valued by those who come. The teaching is geared down to people's real-life situations, and they are enabled to draw on it so that they affirm that their lives are being changed by the gospel and by faith. At the end we hold hands and sing the grace, and the service ends on a high note of praise and thanksgiving and warmth of feeling.

Anointing with oil

It would be logistically impracticable to anoint with oil during the laying on of hands because of the way that activity is spread around the Cathedral. There are also those who affirm that this should be performed only by an ordained person. These matters have been resolved by making this ministry available at the conclusion of the service, when those who have received the laying on of hands and who wish to be anointed come to the communion rails and receive it from our deaconesses. It is an essential part of the healing ministry and represents the recipients' consecration to God and to his purpose for their lives.

Other ministries

Qualified counsellors are available for preliminary counselling. Any who want deeper counselling are asked to make an appointment, so that adequate time can be made available. Prayer requests have been handed in and are then taken by members of the congregation for continuing prayer. By now it is 7.20 p.m., and about half the congregation then move off to their homes or any evening meetings they may wish to attend, while the other half go to the adjoining Chapter House for refreshments, fellowship and a range of ministries such as those provided by books and cassettes. Every other month there is a meeting of the congregation to talk about and decide things in a fully corporate way. There is a variety of other activities both on Wednesdays and at other times, to meet the many needs that people have.

It just isn't possible to put into words all that happens at the healing service; but it is very important to try to give some kind of picture, because this service is where the Spirit of God is working and ministry is taking place, and people are being changed in spirit, mind, body and circumstance. No one knows all that happens, one reason being that we keep a low profile on results. Anything that is of lasting value is what God does, and to him be the praise. Our responsibility is to prepare ourselves and be available, so that we can comfort others with the comfort with which we have been comforted by God.

A prayer
If you would like to join a healing congregation, here is a prayer to say:

Give me Lord, I pray, fellowship with others in the healing ministry. Bless my minister in his role of leadership/bless my congregation in their ministry, that together we may have a ministry of all believers. Thank you for what fellowship I have; I believe it is being extended and added to. Most of all I ask that our Lord will be present in power to save and heal and forgive.

Come to "the Hour of Prayer"
A common feature in most of the big and flourishing Christian churches throughout the world is that the large service on Sunday is complemented by a wide range of small group activities during the week. The service is for

celebration; the group is where the one-to-one ministry takes place in a more detailed way than is usually possible at the bigger meeting. Ideally one should belong to both; each has its part to play.

Small group ministry

We have a number of these groups. Some provide for people living in a particular area, and others focus on a subject. An example of the latter is a group that has been formed recently for those interested in M.S. (multiple sclerosis), which is headed by someone who has been healed of this disease by our ministry. It is called the "Key Group" because a key is the international symbol for work in this area of infirmity, and because we want a positive name rather than one that only refers to the problem.

I would like to refer in more detail to one group we have, because it says a lot about this kind of ministry. It meets each weekday, Monday to Friday, at noon in the Cathedral chapel and is appropriately called "the Hour of Prayer". The number attending would vary between ten and twenty, a larger number being there on Wednesday because it is the day of the healing service, and on Friday when we have the Eucharist and music. As St Andrew's Cathedral is a city church, everyone has had to make a journey to be there, but the sacrifice made is a factor in the blessing received. Some are there nearly every day, others come on certain days, and many come according to the need. Two of our number always come on Tuesday and Wednesday and, after attending the early celebration at eight o'clock, continue all day in intercessory prayer. They handle most of the prayer requests that come in by phone or by post, and one of them is also active in hospital visiting on behalf of the healing ministry.

Although everyone there has his or her own needs, it is noticeable that most of the prayer is for others who are known to those present, or for whom prayer has been asked in one way or another. At the same time, provision is always made to minister to and pray for those who are there, and this is usually done with the laying on of hands and, sometimes, an apposite gift ministry, such as a word of knowledge or discernment. On occasions people come a long distance, even from other states, because they are in need, and because this kind of regular prayer does not operate where they live.

Although it is natural that the subjects for prayer reflect the interests of those who come, we range over a wide area, from the Cathedral ministry in general to industrial and national matters. We seldom finish without praying for the world for which Christ died. Everyone is encouraged to participate, but with our emphasis on the ministry of all believers that presents no problem. Anybody who regularly comes to our activities is used to praying about anything at any time with anyone!

One of the reasons for the Hour of Prayer is that it provides regularity of prayer. We may not be heard for our much speaking, but we are heard for our much believing. The Bible says that we need to "continue in prayer".[27] The bigger the mountain to move, the more there is need for this day-by-day ministry, both for ourselves and for others.

Another important factor is that prayer has an added strength when it is corporate. While nothing takes the place of individual prayer, it is also true that nothing takes the place of corporate prayer. A number of people interceding have more effect than someone on his own. Anyone involved in group prayer knows the wonderful and even surprising answers that come when there is love and faith and united commitment. Here is one such result:

"I am very pleased to be able to express my thanks for the wonderful blessing we have had from my coming to the Cathedral, first to the Hour of Prayer and then to the healing service. For years I had prayed in my own way, but with no real understanding of Christ – but all this has been changed.

"About two and a half years ago the doctors found that my husband had cancer of the larynx. I remember hearing about the healing ministry from a friend a few years before. It was not convenient to come in the evenings, so I started coming nearly every day to the Hour of Prayer. The help I had in every way was incredible, thanks to God and the wonderful ministry in the group. I became increasingly certain that my husband would be cured, to the point that if anyone asked me how he was doing, I told them positively I *knew* he was going to be all right. He is now totally healed and every check shows that he is 100 per cent.

"Now I am thanking God by faith for my husband's commitment to Christ and for the signs of this that I see. I have other wonderful answers to prayer, too many to list, in illness and situations both physical and spiritual.

"I thought I was happy before but did not know what was being missed. It has all been tremendous. I praise and thank God for everything and for Christ in my life." L.R.

I would earnestly advise anyone who has a very big mountain to move to belong to a small group such as is described here and to attend regularly and meaningfully.

A prayer for someone who wishes to join a prayer group

Thank you, Lord Jesus, for your word that where two or three are gathered together in your name you are there in the midst. I believe in faith that you will enable me to have fellowship with others who trust in Christ alone for salvation and who believe that you answer prayer. Lord, I believe you are answering this petition now because it is in your name.

Stay at a healing home

If the advantage of corporate and continuing prayer is seen in a daily prayer group, it is seen even more where it is practised in a residential setting.

We have had a healing home ministry for six months of the year and over a number of years (though not at the present time), in a property that we leased on a beach front within an hour's drive of the Cathedral. As well as being able to stay overnight, people could go for the day and share in the activity, which included prayer and Bible study as well as other pleasures and satisfactions of Christian family life. It was an important centre for counselling, and the phone "ran hot" with requests for prayer.

Agnes Sanford, of happy memory, used to say that water has a therapeutic effect. I am sure that is true. When my own emotional health broke down at an earlier time, I would go for a ferry trip on Sydney harbour, just so that I could hear the sound of the water lapping against the boat. It seemed to communicate a peace that came in no other way.

I am sure that people who came to our healing home had this kind of help too, as they looked through the picture windows or sat in the garden with an "Aussie" beach in front of them and the magnificent Pacific Ocean stretching away to infinity. An afternoon walk up to the headland took in the boating, the rescue helicopter on its pad, the hang-gliders, and the panoramic views of the coastline as far as the eye could see. One of the requirements in this kind of work is that it must be a "silent-salesman".   People need to receive blessing through the setting as well as through the prayers. I want to add that our home was staffed by three senior members of our congregation, who were responsible for the entire ministry. Here is one of the testimonies in our files:

"As a last resort John Hamilton drove his wife Margaret 1,000 kilometres from Queensland to our healing home at Collaroy. She was paralytic with a depression that had lasted a number of years, and which, so far, had not responded to medical treatment. On their arrival it took an hour to persuade her to leave the car and come into the house.

"For the first four weeks we cared for her in a total way; she had to be showered and dressed, fed and humoured. Her only word seemed to be 'no'. At first, she rejected our invitation to attend our Bible study; but in the fifth week she began to show interest in prayer and then welcomed the prayer of faith being shared with her in her room after breakfast. In a gradual way she began to share with the others and join in our family activity.

"Later Margaret went to another healing home for nearly a year, from where we had continued progress reports which praised God for further improvements. Finally she returned to her own home and was able to care fully for her husband. In a progressive way the Lord had given her a great deal of recovery through residential ministries." E.D.

We will not rest until this work is operational in a full-time and permanent way; though I would be lacking in frankness if I did not add that it is easier said than done. Just as the blessing is great, so too is the sacrifice required from those who do the work and provide a ministry that is on duty twenty-four hours a day and seven days a week. It isn't easy to have the right people available in the way that is needed. We thank God for what has happened so far and believe for its further development in the future.

If you are in need and can stay for a time in a healing home, go right ahead. It could make all the difference.

A prayer for a healing home

Lord Jesus, who knew the blessing of an earthly home, bless homes of healing wherever they are situated so that your children can draw on residential ministries of healing and new life. Bless those who have responsibility for such places that they will be upheld by your power and given special grace in every circumstance. May the number of these homes be increased that your kingdom may be extended.

* * *

The two sections of this chapter have been an introduction to those things that a person seeking healing needs to do and draw on. The broad picture that is presented should be seen first. After that, the one who reads will want to choose the parts that are of special help and relevance to him. We are all at different places along the way; in some areas we are relatively advanced, in others we will feel that more progress needs be made, and in some – "tell it not in Gath" (2 Sam. 1:20) – we may be inclined to ask if any progress has been made at all.

May God bless and guide as you read and reflect.

WHAT YOU CAN EXPECT

WHEN THE INSIGHTS presented in the first two chapters are acted on, certain things can be expected to happen. This chapter sets them out. In doing so, it further discusses how the person in need is to react so that he or she finds healing and wholeness.

Recovery can be immediate

The ideal expectation is for perfect healing – there and then. God has promised – we believe – prayer is answered. This, in principle, is the kind of healing which the New Testament records. Those who believe that the commission to preach and heal applies today as well as yesterday, also believe that healing happens in the same way today as yesterday. Jesus said that it will be "according to your faith".[1] Whatever we might think, that is the divine criterion against which our response is to be measured.

Here is an illustration of immediate healing – written by the woman concerned.

"Looking back, I guess I hadn't been completely well since the time I had two difficult pregnancies. Both were full term, but both babies died. This had physical repercussions and it was probably this, so the doctor explained, that led to the positive result in a smear test in 1980. An initial biopsy confirmed abnormal tissue growth, termed severe dysplasia, one stage before cancer.

"I entered hospital for a hysterectomy. With all the

damaged areas removed, and with the bladder re-
positioned, I was told I would feel like a new woman
within a few months. With some ten years of mediocre
health behind me, I looked forward to that prospect with
relief and expectancy.

"It didn't happen. There were long-term effects from
the anaesthetic and I was plagued with infection after
infection. I just dragged myself through 1981 and fought a
battle both physically and psychologically. By the time I
entered hospital for a second major operation, I had had a
year of disturbed, painful nights, long aching mornings
and afternoons in bed to regain strength for the evenings.
Still, this operation was to fix everything. The bladder was
to be re-shaped and the infected part removed.

"Once again the effects of the anaesthetic were
devastating and mending was slow and painful. The
discomfort, particularly on going to the toilet, remained
extreme. The next consultation was three months after the
operation and I shall always remember it was Monday, 8th
February, 1982. The ligaments which cause the pelvis to
contract after childbirth were diagnosed as being severely
infected, and I was told I would have to go back into
hospital to be bound up and immobilised for six months.

"I reached breaking point that night, and wept
helplessly as I tried to go to sleep. A real sense of
worthlessness overcame me. I felt a failure as a wife and
mother and a complete waste of space on this earth. I
wanted it all to end, and cried out to God to kill me or heal
me – it didn't really matter which. Amazingly I came out of
that brokenness refreshed and with the absolute conviction that if I went to the healing service at St Andrew's
Cathedral I would be healed.

"We had heard that there was a healing ministry at the
Cathedral, but knew nothing about it at all, so we phoned
and found that there was a service held every Wednesday at
6.00 p.m. Today was Tuesday; I counted the hours.
Wednesday afternoon arrived at last. I had a sleep to
muster up the energy to travel, and at last the time came to
leave.

"We arrived at the healing service, and the first thing that impressed us was the incredible atmosphere of the place – so warm and loving. The service began and was so joyful, the people really were praising the Lord. We felt we had come home. I was just beginning to feel the strain of sitting upright when the invitation was given to those who wanted prayer to raise their hands. Up shot mine and a quite ordinary, gentle sort of fellow rose from among those sitting near and laid his hand on my head. He asked my need and when I told him, he prayed a simple prayer of thanks!

"I truly felt that Jesus had passed by and that I had touched the hem of his garment. The rest of the service passed in a warm blur. Then I was anointed with oil.

"I had been completely healed. I felt a warm vibrating feeling in my hips which contracted a whole 'size'. I stood for over an hour chatting with people without feeling the least strain. We went to dinner afterwards to celebrate and drank red wine. What a thrill to someone who had trouble drinking orange juice! There has been no more infection, no more acute discomfort, no more of the debilitating ill health I had for years.

"But the most wonderful thing of all was the realisation that God really is our Father and does care about us. That Jesus is our Lord, Saviour and Friend and that he heals today just as he did yesterday. This is not the end of my testimony, it is the beginning of a whole new relationship with God for my family and me.

"It is now over a year since I was healed and I feel younger and fitter than ever. Our lives have been further transformed by the fullness of the Holy Spirit and each day has become a fresh adventure with the Lord.

"Thank you Lord, that you cared even for me." V.C.

Recovery can be gradual

For reasons that we are now going to examine, healing can be gradual. We need to understand the factors that contribute to this, so that where our response is inadequate, we can remedy that defect if it is possible to do so. This will be a more intelligent and productive approach than the common practice of passing off the lack of answer to prayer by attributing it to "God's will".

Not that we are in any way unconcerned about "God's will". On the contrary, we have been at pains to begin at that point and affirm that the broad themes of scriptural promise *reveal* God's will to us. It is because there is a clear promise that "the prayer offered in faith will make the sick person well",[2] that we should think it possible that where prayer has been unanswered it may not be to do with God's part, but with ours. (By "ours" we mean that of the sick person and the church.) Where it is a case of what Jesus referred to as "the littleness of your faith"[3] (a reference to his closest followers), it is not so much a question of "God can, but will he?" but rather of "God will, but can he?"

With this in mind, let us now look at temporary or progressive answer to prayer for healing in an enquiring and positive frame of mind.

"My healing didn't last"

Some years ago, when in the United States, I had contact with a woman who had been ministered to by Kathryn Kuhlman. She had drawn upon remarkable healing of cancer, so much so that it had become front page news in the press, but now the problem was returning. "My healing didn't last," she told me.

And recently, as I was walking through St Andrew's Cathedral, a young man approached me and said that he had come to the healing service a fortnight previously because he was a chronic asthma sufferer, and that he had been prayed for with the laying on of hands. He had been much better during the following week, but now his condition was getting back to what it was like before. He was mystified; obviously there had been a response to prayer, but the improvement had not been maintained.

This happens sometimes in my counselling ministry. At the end of an interview I always believe with my visitor(s) for healing or whatever is the relevant provision of God. Then I arrange for him (or her) to come to see me again, so that the matter can be followed through. On the subsequent occasion, he may be full of gratitude for the change for the better that has followed the earlier visit, but within another week or ten days the sickness has begun to assert itself again.

Some of the reasons

Before we go any further, it is worth saying that healing isn't the only blessing from God that does not always seem to last. The many who go through the solemn rite of Confirmation and who are never seen again, or who quickly fall away, are a well known and glaring example. The plain fact is that "the pilgrim way" is littered with blessings from God that have quickly come and quickly gone. What Jesus said about the seed sown in shallow or stony ground surely has some application. The fault is not in the seed – be it healing or salvation – but in the ground in which it was planted; there is something inadequate in our appropriation of what God gives. If the truth be told, we all have areas in our Christian experience where we are shallow ground.

At this point, the question I referred to earlier (see page 32) needs to be asked of some people: do they really *want* to get well? Might their partial blessing be because of their partial response?

What is more pertinent to the average person is that the improvement drawn on may well come from the faith that has been exercised on his or her *behalf*, either in the healing service or in counselling. This is good as far as it goes, but sooner or later (and the sooner the better) the sick person must learn to make his own faith response if healing is to be drawn on in a continuing and complete way.

Faith for others is like a blood transfusion; it may be necessary and has a wonderful result, but it cannot continue indefinitely. It is a boost designed to get the sick man on his own feet. Prayer for others is a faith "transfusion" with the same strengths and limitations. This is worth thinking about.

Another common reason why blessing can decrease is that the person is asking the question, "I wonder if it will last?" Often he is hoping for the best but fearing the worst. He may be living on a knife-edge, with faith and praise on one side and doubt and fear on the other. That lurking fear may be something he doesn't want to admit or express, but if it is there, that, more than anything else, is why sickness returns. In what the Mary Sisters refer to as "the battle of faith", so often it is fear that wins out – and we know the consequence of having that destructive companion.

Take more of the medicine

Assuming that the possible explanations above have been worked through, we can now move ahead in a constructive way. If the sick person has shown some improvement, however partial and transitory, it means that he has drawn on healing in degree. It shows that healing is available in response to faith, and he should be greatly encouraged.

Secondly, it is obvious that he has not drawn on as much healing as he needs. We need to realise that there can be a contest, if that is the right word, between sickness and healing. We might think of the sickness as being the sea-shore and healing coming in like the tide. Sometimes it does not come in far enough or doesn't go deep enough or, for one reason or another (we have given a number of them), it isn't maintained. There is also a tendency for the tide to go out, because sickness is a living force; unless it is rooted out completely and in permanence, it will re-assert itself.

If for any reason healing has not been received in as complete a way as is needed, we will tend to find the sickness taking over again. This can be a see-saw activity. When this happens, we need to react in a positive way and re-affirm our healing. Something of what can happen for good has been seen, and we need "to take more of the medicine". That is, we are to react to what remains of the problem by continuing to draw on the answer. If the lack of perfect healing has meant that we have reverted to being problem-centred in our thinking, we need to become answer-centred again – by faith.

Some people find this easier to do the second time round. They have been encouraged by what has happened; they have an added understanding of what they need to do, and they are ready to persevere in prayer. Others find it more difficult. At first their faith had a simple child-like quality about it that brought at least some immediate blessing, but as they seek to continue in faith they tend to strive, and that is counter-productive. It is helpful to remember here that there is "joy and peace in believing".[4] This is why the prayer that praises God is always the most effective way to exercise faith, whether it be when we pray at first, or in an on-going way.

It might well be that more outside faith should be drawn on. If so, go to a healing service and receive the laying on of hands, which allows other people to add their believing faith to yours. Don't hesitate to do this, provided you are striking a right balance between drawing on the faith of others and developing your own.

As we continue in prayer, it frequently happens that things come into focus which need to be dealt with, and which so far have not been thought of in the context of healing: the need to forgive and be forgiven, the need to face past hurts and receive the healing of the memories, the need to believe for wholeness in other related areas. These have been referred to already, but they need to be seen in this setting. It is rather like repairing an old house; you fix up one part and that reveals more trouble. Don't be put off by this; there is no reason why it cannot all be brought into good condition, but it will take time and application.

If you would think of the sickness as being a horizontal line, and immediate and permanent healing being a line that is vertical and at right angles to it, the kind of healing we are talking about is a line that rises from the horizontal at an angle of, shall we say, forty-five degrees. But it is more complicated than that; the ascending line will have rises in it that represent the degree of healing being drawn on, and falls that represent the recurring symptoms of sickness. The line is rising generally because we are reacting to any remaining symptoms in a positive and not a negative way. For the same reason the rises will become more frequent and will last longer, and the falls will be less frequent and have shorter duration, until we finally come on to a level where there is no return of the sickness at all.

Faith is a decision of the mind

To get these things right in a consistent way requires that we get our faith-thinking right every day. I spend time every morning doing this until my mind is "ticking over" in a positive and believing way. It is so easy to be affirming the problem and not the answer, even when one has come to faith on previous occasions. Our mind is a very unruly member, and we can never assume that it will react in faith and praise. Left to itself, it is more likely a case of "I do not do the good I want, but the evil I do not want is what I do".[5] When I get it wrong so that the problem is being affirmed, I endeavour to learn from the mistake, so that my reactions in similar circumstances later on will be more effective.

Let us sum up what has been said.

Instead of saying, "My healing didn't last", concentrate on thanking God for what blessing there is, or as the Bible puts it so succinctly, "Continue in prayer, and watch in the same with thanksgiving".[6] This means that we are not to react negatively to any remaining or returning symptoms of sickness, but believe for *further* healing. St Paul gives us the right word of encouragement, "He who began a good work in you will bring it to completion".[7]

Assuming that time is on our side and that we are doing this with others – we with them and they with us – there is no limit to the healing that can be drawn on from God in a cumulative way. With this in mind, I share with you a further text that is my rule of life and ministry, "Let steadfastness (patience) have its full effect, that you may be perfect and complete, lacking in nothing".[8]

A prayer for someone who is getting well gradually

Father, I thank you for what blessing has been drawn on so far. To get a touch from the Lord is so real. As I watch in prayer with thanksgiving, I know you are being enabled to complete that which you have begun. For what healing there is by sight I praise your name, and for the healing that is affirmed by faith, again, "praise your name". Bless those who pray for me, that together we will increase in the reality of your "here and now" kingdom, through Jesus our Lord.

Moving the bigger mountains

Many people who draw on divine healing have problems that are long-standing and in an advanced state. Sometimes that is why they come; they have tried everything else, and this is their last resort. That is not a criticism – but it is a factor that has to be taken into account. Some have illnesses that, humanly speaking, are terminal.

In this section we consider what can be done, or not done, in these circumstances. We begin with reservations and go on to explain what is meant by sacrificial prayer and how it is exercised. Our approach is conservative, but positive.

Reservations

When someone approaches me about healing who has what might be called "a bigger mountain" to move, I talk the matter over with him and his family in a frank and sensitive way.

It is necessary to make the point that, just as the more advanced the illness is, the more difficult it is for medical treatment to be effective, so too it is more difficult for prayer to be effective. I do not "go out on a limb" and speak about the promise of healing in an unqualified way. This is not to say that God cannot heal; but the size of the mountain has to be taken into account, as do the limits of our faith.

Another part of the whole is that the time comes to each of us when we are to depart this life. Then one does not pray for healing, but for grace to leave this world for the next in a way that befits the person who is trusting in Christ for eternal life. But until that point is reached, I believe healing is available in the same way as the medical resource is available, and our approach to both should be the same.

When we have talked the matter through, I say that within the limitations the circumstances impose, I will help the patient in any way possible, and I set no limit to what God is able to do. Sick people are used to their medical advisers discussing their condition and the available options in a balanced and helpful way, and they should have the same kind of experience when they come to the church to enquire about the healing ministry. Assuming that, I find that people understand and accept what is said in a mature and positive way.

Agnes Sanford, who was the world authority on the Christian healing ministry, strongly affirmed that one did not automatically pray for healing for every sick person who came across one's path. Because faith is what we are responsible to God for, and again, having in mind the extent of the problem many people have, she would wait on God before committing herself to believe for healing in any particular situation. She often commented that many people who followed her guidelines about healing nevertheless did not follow her on this point. As time goes by, I see and appreciate more of what she said, and both advocate and practise the restraint she advised on this important matter.

Soaking prayer

Given the above, the principles of persevering prayer need to be clearly understood and acted on with a blend of discipline, courage and a reliance on the guidance of the Holy Spirit. Francis MacNutt illustrates what this means with interesting and instructive data in his book, *The Power to Heal*.[9] When prayer is made for two minutes there can be minimal change; after fifteen minutes it is more obvious; and after an hour the miraculous is fully apparent. And so on.

This is what is meant and accomplished by fasting. There is no virtue in merely doing without food; that only makes one hungry and miserable. But when ones uses the sensation of being without food to provide a continuing stimulus or reminder to be believing God for his blessing, its intended purpose is being served. And far from it being distressing, one quickly comes to an elevated level of communion with God and praise of his holy name that is not drawn on in any other way. Time takes on a new dimension, as one only wants the experience to last and not to end.

The hair-shirt worn by some of the ancients had the same intention. The irritation was deliberately induced to give them a moment by moment reminder to be depending on God more. In passing, it is interesting to note that when Archbishop Thomas à Becket was martyred, he was found to be wearing this garment next to his skin, which prompted the monks to exclaim that he was a saint.[10]

One can also react to sickness and circumstance in the same way. I can vouch for this through my own experience. When, at last, I came to an awareness that, as far as God was concerned, I did not have to be afraid, I then went on to accept the soundness of mind that it was his will for me to have. But this worked only for as long as it took to make the affirmation. When it finished, the fears were waiting to sweep over me again, and they did. Some progress had been made, but much more was needed.

This came in an unexpected way. One day I was so at the

end of myself with anxiety that I decided to get away from it all for a while and see a film. For two hours and more my mind was filled with the story and music of *Oliver!* When it had finished and I came out of the cinema, to my great surprise and relief everything was wonderfully different. I didn't have a fear in the world. I remember saying to myself, "This must be what life is like without fear!" But the act of bringing it to mind seemed to resurrect the problem, and within a short time it was the same as before.

Put healing in place of sickness

But I had had an experience. This time my fears had been left behind, not just for a moment, but for two hours. Why? Because my mind had been filled with something else – a film. I couldn't go on doing that, and didn't want to. So what else would do the same thing? What better than the power and love and soundness of mind that God wanted me to have? It meant that not only did I accept this provision (I had done that already in a beginning way), but it became what I affirmed in a *continuing* way.

As long as my conscious mind was filled with my continuing affirmations, I had relative peace of mind, but if for any reason they stopped, the fear automatically took over. It was as simple as that. It meant that I had to turn my day into one long affirmation of faith. I reached the point where I was doing this for literally every moment without so much as putting in a comma; before I was out of bed in the morning, while brushing my teeth, driving my car and, with a corner of my mind, whatever else I was doing. Not that I was any better at the day's end, but if nothing else I wasn't worse, which was different from what it had been like up till then. At least I was no longer just giving in to the problem because I did not know what else to do; now I was fighting it with the answer given by God.

The next day the problem was still there, as though the previous day's affirmations hadn't existed. I continued to react positively, because I had to; it was no virtue on my part, it was an exercise in self-survival. Not infrequently I was holding on for dear life. "Thank you, Father, you are healing me now . . ."

More than in any other way, I expressed my faith by praising God – for what he had done, was doing, and would do: "Thank you, Father, for what you have done through Jesus. Thank you for the promises you have made. Thank you for your love which casts out fear. Praise be to the Holy Spirit who is giving me healing now. Glory be to the Father and to the Son and to the Holy Spirit. Praise God, praise God, praise God . . ."

As I continued to do this – not day in and week out, but month after month – it gradually came through to me that the clouds were shifting and blue skies were beginning to peep through. For short times I could stop my prayer of faith and no fear came; when it returned, I would go back to filling my mind with all the fullness of God in the way that has been described. If you like, the positive was being put in place of the negative. But it was much more than positive thinking; I was believing by faith for God's promised blessing so that I did not doubt in my heart.

It was a tremendous encouragement to find that my persevering prayer was gradually being effective. In a word, healing was increasing and sickness was decreasing. Finally and at long last, and directly as a result of what has been set out in this book and especially in this chapter, I came out on to a plateau where my lifelong fears which had brought me to breakdown had disappeared – and disappeared so completely that they never so much as come to mind, unless by a deliberate act of recall for the purpose of giving testimony to the healing that God gives through prayer and fasting.

From death to life

In case there are those who feel that this can be done for an emotional condition but not for something physical, the following account is included.

A Christian social worker at the Royal Alexandra Hospital for Children, Sydney, referred Tom and Marcia

Burrows to me, hoping that I might be able to help them. Their infant daughter, aged twelve months, was critically ill with leukaemia and not expected to live. Tom and Marcia will not mind my saying that they had only a slender involvement in the Christian religion, and no understanding whatsoever of the healing ministry.

I visited them in the hospital, and realised that Angela was very close to death. As has been said already, I do not feel free to pray for healing with no reservation in this kind of situation. But things didn't work out according to my preconceived position. The parents' love for their little girl, and the trust they immediately placed in me, led them to ask and press me to pray for healing. Short of walking out on them, I could not avoid their plea. Very much against my better judgment I prayed for healing, and because of that felt obliged to follow the matter through. When I subsequently mentioned this to one of our office staff, who is also committed to the healing ministry, she too took up the challenge, which again left me with no alternative but to do my part as best I could.

I visited the baby every day for a month to pray over her in faith, and my prayer partner was equally diligent in her support. For some time Angela hovered in the balance, and then very, very slowly began to improve. The gradual improvement continued, and by the end of the month she had gone into remission and subsequently was discharged from hospital.

Five years have gone by with no recurrence of the disease, and her physicians describe her condition as being "in complete remission". With her parents and a baby brother she lives in one of our Sydney suburbs, and it is a joy to hear from them at Christmas time with their loving and grateful greeting. And, perhaps not surprisingly, Angela has a very special relationship with God. Her mother says that "she walks with Jesus".

Reflections

I am not being defensive in saying that the pastoral

position I take up is intended to be conservative. Perhaps it is for this reason that sometimes the thing that is a "breakthrough" is learnt accidentally. It is when one is pushed through the mind-barrier that has been set according to our present level of understanding and experience, that further knowledge is gained.

When I reflect on Angela's story, I ask myself: do we give up too easily? Something else that we fail to consider is that one needs time to pray and minister in this sacrificial way. Often I feel my butter is spread too thinly, because of the number of people to whom I am giving pastoral care. There is a good argument for ministering to fewer people and in more depth.

Moving the bigger mountains: balance is the important thing; and sacrificial prayer; and willingness to be taken further forward.

A prayer to move a bigger mountain

Blessed Lord, who prayed all night when the need was great, help me to pray all day for my great need and give me of your wisdom that I will pray aright. I believe that as my prayer of faith continues, you are casting my mountain into the sea, spadeful by spadeful. I have faith to affirm that in the best and truest sense your will is being done on earth as it is in heaven and that, in this difficulty, I and mine are being changed into your likeness more and more. Lord Jesus, my hand is in yours; I will not let you go unless you bless me.

Healing leads to wholeness

As we draw on healing, whether it be immediate or gradual, and as we are concerned with moving bigger mountains, we will find that healing leads to wholeness. By healing, we mean the healing of the immediate circumstances about which we are praying; by wholeness, we mean the healing of everything that is relevant to our well-being.

The point I would make, and with considerable
emphasis, is that healing cannot be looked at in isolation.
If it is, it may well be short-lived, even if it is drawn on.
And when healing is short-lived, it is not so easy to draw
on the second time round. Perhaps the most important
thing in all that we are saying is that we need wholeness *as
well as* healing. That is the message of the Christian
healing ministry.

Profit from what has happened
The first thing to think about is that we must profit
from what has happened. I believe strongly in what the
medical researchers, who have been quoted earlier in the
book, have said in this connection. In as far as we can
reasonably think that there have been background
causative factors in our illness, we not only need to believe
for their healing, but also to take steps to see that they do
not recur at a later time. That is, we will in future
discipline our minds and feelings to react in terms of the
relevant answer God provides, and not in terms of the
stress. It is important to know that subsequent stress can
come from an entirely different source, but it can activate
the same Achilles' heel or weak spot in our physical and
emotional make-up.

Once we have had a sickness experience, it is easier to
have it back again than it was to have it in the first place.
(Obviously this does not apply when one has had, for
example, an appendicectomy; the reference is to sickness
or injuries that are capable of renewal.) This only stands to
reason. As a youth, I went camping and once managed to
drive an axe into my leg. Thereafter I had to be careful not
to knock that leg because of the weakness left by the injury.
If we have drawn on healing in any way, including that
given specifically by the Holy Spirit, we need to take care,
especially at first, not to expose ourselves to more stress
than we are able to tolerate.

Wholeness is more than healing

The second requirement grows out of the first. We have to be concerned with wholeness. We cannot divide ourselves up into compartments so that we are practising healing in one of them and allowing sickness-making activity to run riot in another. Our whole life needs to profit from our experience, so that we believe for wholeness in ourselves, in others and in our environment. This should not come as any surprise to followers of Christ, because that is what Christianity is all about. God is not concerned only to clear up one room of our house; he will certainly go on through every room and every grubby corner until all things are made new.

If we don't have this approach, then healing, whether it be from prayer or medicine, will be like putting plaster over an infection. The illness may well recur at a later time in the same or in a different form.

Make healing a way of life

The third point is a further development: make healing a way of thought and a way of life. Let me refer again to the parents of the boy who was a hunchback, and who drew on healing through their remarkable faith and vision. As I got to know them I found, to my surprise, that they did not pray in the "usual" way. When I commented on this, they gave an interesting and revealing reply. They said that they were not in any way opposed to overt prayer, but didn't want to give the impression that it was something put into words *at a particular time*. For them it was like the air that they breathed. It was the way they lived their life; it was their thought and response moment by moment. It was "the real them", if you know what I am trying to say.

If this sounds refreshingly different, let me tell you something else that had an equal influence on my personal life and public ministry.

After reading *The Cross and the Switchblade* by David Wilkerson, I went, at a later time, to visit Teen Challenge in Brooklyn, New York, where he had begun his work of ministering to drug addicts and others for whom no effective community resource was available. David's brother Don was responsible for the Centre at the time, and as he was in conference when I arrived, he arranged for me to be shown over the complex until he was free. In the course of being shown around, I met a number of fellows who were in the Intake Centre. (The Intake Centre for girls was in another place, and I did not have the opportunity to go there.)

Two things struck me. The first was the lurid backgrounds of these young men. You name it, they had done it – drugs, crime, sex, alcohol and other things, some of which I had never heard of before. The second point was that these young fellows were like "the boy next door". They were upright in bearing, courteous in manner, and (very noticeably) compassionate to one another. I am not exaggerating; they were like the best products from our church schools.

I was intrigued and nonplussed. How could these two characteristics be reconciled? When the opportunity came, I talked this over with Don Wilkerson – to find that the explanation was simplicity itself, and something that fitted closely into my own evangelical background.

In brief, Christ was presented to these men as Saviour and Healer, and they were called on to accept him for every need they had. This meant that they accepted Christ as their Saviour and they accepted Christ as their Healer. If they were alcoholics, they accepted Christ for the healing of their alcoholism in the same way as they accepted Christ for the forgiveness of their sins. That is, they accepted their healing, they made a decision to that end, and they affirmed what they had done by faith. This is what I have been saying, and this is where I learned it.

Subsequent to this, they would go through the trauma of withdrawal when they had a craving to return to alcohol or whatever the problem was that they had to begin with. At this point, members of the staff, and others who were more advanced in the programme, would stand by the one going through withdrawal, supporting him in his new-found faith, and affirming with him and for him the healing that was being believed for. Even when they were at the end of their tether, they would continue to affirm their blessing by faith.

Because of this persevering, sacrificial and vicarious prayer, the person concerned would finally come through, so that the old cravings no longer had sway over his life. Instead he had the wholeness of Christ in the ways that were needed. Complementing this, he then went into a programme of re-education, so that he became rooted and grounded in the Christian faith and life. This full-time programme lasted, in all, about nine months.

By their fruits shall they be known. The success rate of those who went through the Teen Challenge programme was of the order of 86 per cent, which is a far, far better result than any other programme of rehabilitation for these kinds of problems.

All or nothing at all

A further and equally important point about their practice of ministry was that their acceptance of healing was affirmed in a *total* kind of way. There were no half measures.

It so happened that the reason why Don Wilkerson could not meet me when I first arrived was that he was in the process of dismissing a man who was on the programme, but was not fitting into their rules. Believe it or not, all he had been guilty of was continuing to talk to others about his former life. But the problem was really a matter of fundamental importance, because in effect he was keeping his own and other men's problems going, preventing from being fully effective the healing that he and they were, at the same time, professing and needing. He wanted it both ways. But it didn't work both ways. It only worked when he was willing to switch over to his new life with no reservation at all. Given that, he would have become "a new creation",[11] which was the explanation

for the extraordinary "before and after" stories of Teen
Challenge, New York.

This is what we have been saying about getting well
again. We have to switch over from the problem to the
answer in that same kind of way. While the problems of
men and women at Teen Challenge may well be different
from those most of us have, the principle of healing and
the principle of discipline required are the same. Three-
quarters of the reason why the Christian answer doesn't
work as it should is that we do not apply it in the
thoroughgoing and whole-hearted way that it needs to be
applied. G.K. Chesterton's famous words are relevant, "It
is not that Christianity has been weighed in the balance
and found wanting. It has been found to be difficult and
therefore not tried." It is for good reason that Jesus said
that, if we were going to be effective in the new life, the old
life had to be put to death. And this concerns healing as
well. The problems need to be crucified with Christ, and
we need to believe in a complete and total way.

The most important part of wholeness

An essential requirement, if we are to have wholeness as
well as healing, is that we believe on Christ for salvation,
and have his presence and power in our lives. Before this
happens we are lost, but afterwards we are found; before,
we are dead in our sins, afterwards we are alive unto God;
before, Christ is a figure in history, afterwards he is our
mighty and ever-living Saviour. It isn't enough to be a
church-goer or to obey "the Golden Rule" or to have
healing or anything else; we must have the living Christ in
our lives and trust in him only to be made right with the
Father.

Enough has been said already as to how one draws on
this blessing. What remains to be done is to say the sinner's
prayer. Here it is: "Father in heaven, I acknowledge that I
am a sinner and have fallen short of your standards in so
many ways. I believe that Jesus died for my sins on the
cross and rose again from the dead to make me to be at one

with you. I now accept Christ as my own personal Saviour. This is my decision and I affirm it by faith. By your grace I will now walk in your way all my life until it comes to my turn to stand before you and receive the crown of everlasting life. In the name of the Father, and of the Son and of the Holy Spirit, Amen."

If you have made this prayer your own, then do three things:

Tell someone what you have done.

Begin to pray and read the scriptures and, if you do not do so already, attend Christian worship.

Remember that Satan is the accuser of the brethren. If he tempts you to think nothing has changed, make this reply, "Get behind me, Satan. I affirm by faith that Jesus Christ is my Saviour. Praise God!" Keep making this affirmation until you have a conviction given by the Holy Spirit that you are his and he is yours for ever.

And not least, have in mind that what has been said about the completeness of our response which is needed for healing applies in exactly the same way for salvation. All areas of our Christian experience can be on the surface, but wholeness goes all the way through.

A prayer for wholeness

Blessed Lord Christ, I hear your words, "Would you be made whole?" and my response is, "Yes, Lord, make me whole in spirit, mind and body. Make me whole in relationships so that I have total Christian oneness with everyone – yes, everyone. And most of all, make me 'complete in Christ.'" In his name I pray.

Is death failure?

A minority of those who are prayed for are healed at once;

the majority of those who are healed are healed gradually. There are those who are healed partially; and there are those who are not healed physically, but who have a healing of the spirit.

There are also those who are prayed for and who die. Whether or not this latter experience is part of what one expects, it is part of what can happen, and we need to talk about it in an open way from experience.

One comment made by critics is that such faith as they and their family have will be adversely affected by such an outcome, so that the last stage is worse than the first. While this point is frequently made in a theoretical way because it seems logical, it is also true that instances are sometimes quoted that support this position. Before going further, let me say again that our considerable experience shows that this is not a problem for those individuals and their families who are members of a soundly-based and pastorally active healing ministry congregation.

Let me share with you a story from our pastoral casebook which will bring into focus what we have learned in this connection.

John and Libby Galston called me on the phone to say that their young son Mark was critically ill in the Children's Hospital; they had read my book, *Your Healing Is Within You*, and could I help in any way with the healing ministry? The matter was obviously urgent, so we arranged a time, and they were in my office within an hour or so of their first telephoning.

At an earlier time their little boy, aged nine, had complained of headaches, and ultimately he was diagnosed as having a brain tumour. This had been removed by a surgical procedure, and he was able to resume his ordinary activity, including going to school. But there had been a reappearance of his symptoms at this later time, and a recurrence of the tumour had been diagnosed. Their medical specialist said that if Mark was his child he would not let him have a further operation, and advised against it. He said the only help that could be given was palliative, and they would keep Mark comfortable with sedation. He was unconscious at the present time, and his parents were awaiting the end.

I explained to them sensitively and carefully the reservations I have about exercising the healing ministry in these circumstances, and said that provided they understood this, I would help in any way that was possible. I said that I would be prepared to pray in a positive way about healing, provided we were open to any further guidance that God might be pleased to give. They were perfectly happy for us to proceed in this way, and together we went to the hospital to visit their son. He was in a coma. Everything that could be done for him medically had been done. We took our places around his bedside, rested our hands lightly on his arms, and I prayed: "Our loving Father in heaven, we know that you have a special love for children because Jesus called them to him, and we know that your love and provision for Mark is perfect in both this life and the next. We lay our hands on him as a sign of our faith and our love, and pray that you will give him all the healing that can be given. We do not know all that you have for him, but we would be channels of your perfect blessing for his life, and we believe you are using our faith so that our Lord Jesus Christ is glorified in Mark and in us. By faith we praise you for answering our prayer in Jesus' name."

I anointed him with holy oil, and we prayed the Lord's Prayer together and said the grace.

The next day, to the incredulity of the hospital staff, Mark came out of his coma and was in full possession of his faculties, though still confined to his bed. The transformation of this little boy from what he had been like the previous day could only be described as miraculous. We thanked God for his blessing, and continued to believe that he was showing us more of his will and provision for Mark.

We hadn't long to wait. When I subsequently visited him, I found that he was rather a demanding little boy and wanted this and that done for him. At first I met his requests, but when I didn't measure up to exactly what he wanted, he began to abuse me and used some very bad language. I put up with this for a while, until one day I walked out on him and could hear him shouting even after I had left the ward. I remember asking him on one occasion at this time whether he loved Jesus, but this only brought forth another outburst.

It was obvious that he was very disturbed, and his behaviour was a sign and symptom of someone who was trying to call attention, albeit in an asocial way, to an inner and unresolved need.

I met with his parents, who were delightful people and obviously embarrassed because of what was happening. In reply to my questions, they said he had been a happy and well-adjusted child until a younger sister was born, and then he began to "play up". In particular he was hostile towards his mother and would sometimes throw stones at her. I explained to them that the coming of his younger sister had "put his nose out of joint", so to speak, and that his aggressive behaviour was a way of trying to get the attention which he had been used to before his sister came, and which he now *felt* he was being deprived of. The ministry he needed was that of inner healing, and we prayed to that end: "We believe that you are coming into Mark's life, making up for the love that he *feels* he hasn't got, and enabling him to be healed and made mature in his relationships with his family and with everyone else."

I disciplined my mind to react to the difficulties by affirming the answer by faith and on his behalf. Two other members of our congregation were visiting him by now, and we believed this together, as did his parents.

Perhaps I should explain at this point that Mark's mother, Libby, was a devout Roman Catholic, and the children had been baptised in that church; the father, John, was a nominal Anglican. The Roman Catholic chaplain was faithfully visiting Mark and ministering to his parents, and he was more than pleased for me to be playing my part. It was a practical illustration of the ministry from two churches combining and complementing one another in the interests of this little boy.

As we continued to affirm the inner healing that he needed, and disciplined ourselves to react to any problem behaviour in this positive way, he began to quieten down, until after several weeks he finally became a normal and charming little fellow.

By now he was calling me Uncle Jim, and I reached the point of asking him again if he loved the Lord Jesus. He wasn't sure how to go about this, so I said to him that Jesus first loved us and we are just returning his love. He smiled and showed he understood. Shortly after, he was confirmed in his church; I attended the service and was asked to be one of his sponsors. It was a wonderfully happy and uplifting occasion with other members of his family present, and was followed by a party afternoon tea, which had been thoughtfully prepared by the hospital staff. After that the religious Sister brought him Holy Communion regularly. He said to me one day (this was not a reference to Holy Communion), "Jesus comes to visit me and he sits over there." He was happy and in perfect harmony with Jesus and the members of his family and with everyone else.

On a Sunday morning, some six weeks after his parents had first approached me, I received an urgent phone call from his father asking me to come as soon as possible. When I was free from my duties at the Cathedral, I went to the hospital. The boy was deeply unconscious, and his parents and I knew that God's redemptive work had been done and that the time had come for Mark to go and be with the Lord. We committed him to Jesus who had given such a wonderful experience of healing, and we felt God's presence with us and specially with Mark. At five o'clock that afternoon he moved peacefully into eternal life.

After the funeral, his parents, who had come to the healing service throughout the time of his illness, came again with his brothers and sisters and sat in the front row.

Their smiling faces were a testimony of God's blessing in the midst of their bereavement. And John now attends Holy Communion regularly in the Cathedral at our weekday services. "All this has brought me back to God," he said quietly and meaningfully.

The principle of the above story could be repeated many times over. We have found that where prayer is made over someone who subsequently dies, his life span is wonderfully extended, and during that time he is prepared for eternity by the Holy Spirit. As well as his own needs being met, so too are the needs of those who are near and dear to him. When this has been done, he quietly goes to be with Christ. And everyone knows and says there has been a blessing that only God can give.

Far from the healing ministry being destructive when the person concerned subsequently dies, it enables blessing to be there that transforms death into Christian victory. Surely there is healing in that too.

A prayer

O blessed Christ, I ask for your ministry to prepare me for that day when I leave this world and stand before the King. If that preparation is to come through some permitted difficulty, I submit to that trial that I be chastened and refined so that my imperfections are left behind. I am in so great need of holiness. O, holy Jesus, cleanse me I pray.

Out of the waters of affliction and trusting only in Christ's finished work, O Judge eternal, I come.

*   *   *

What has been written is intended to be a balanced account of what you can expect when you draw on the healing ministry in the fellowship of the church. But even so, it isn't easy to capture the spirit and detail of what happens. The appendix that follows takes the matter further by allowing members of the congregation to speak for themselves. Their testimonies support and fill out what has already been said and are an inspiring demonstration of what God does when the insights that have been presented are taught and believed.

APPENDICES TO PART I

WHAT YOU CAN EXPECT AT A HEALING SERVICE

Just before this book was written, members of the healing ministry congregation at St Andrew's Cathedral, Sydney, were invited to give written answers to a series of questions designed to enable them to say what the service and ministry meant to them. The importance of this lies in the fact that these people are the ones who, in a special way, have put the healing ministry to the test. Their replies have not been edited in any way, and no answer or comment has been left out because it was different in principle from those that are printed.

Here are the questions and a very small cross-section of the answers given.

Question 1: What help has the healing ministry been to you?

"It has completely changed my life." S.F.

"Each day has been turned from a dull routine into victorious joy." D.B.

"No matter how 'down' I feel when I go, I always come away strengthened and enabled to face up to life." N.T.

"As a result of coming I have been shown the way of salvation." S.B.

"No answer is adequate; it is immeasurable." R.B.

"I was profoundly moved by the informality and untraditional format of the service; the spontaneity of the prayers gives the impression of direct contact with God in a real and meaningful way and has enabled me to see God anew." J.H.

"Completely stopped a deep fear of cancer." L.B.

"The healing ministry showed me what I had been seeking all my life – the fullness of life in Christ Jesus." L.R.

"So many other healing ministries appear to concentrate on physical results. This is a ministry of wholeness for body, mind and spirit and relationships. It is a teaching-based ministry which had opened the scriptures and given me a whole new understanding of how God wants me to live. It has shown me that I am meant to take God's promises literally and act on them." H.G.

"It has given me healing in bereavement." P.R.

"Immense amounts of time have been given to us in wise, compassionate counselling." M.L.

"After going to the healing service in August 1981 for the first time, my husband and I found our lives changed – our marriage was healed and we found a new life together and with the Lord." T.C.

Question 2: Have you, or has someone you know well, been healed by God? Give details.

"I have had back problems since the age of eight after falling out of a tree. After sixteen years of pain I came to the healing service and one year later am playing tennis and ten pin bowling." B.C.

"In 1957 my first baby died after a tragic accident. My grief was suppressed at the time and over the years covered well and truly. At a healing service in the Cathedral in July 1982, the Reverend Don Douglass preached a sermon on 'Stop Passing the Buck'. He said we can go on making excuses for our behaviour because of past experiences or we can ask for healing of memories and stop being bound by the past. I knew that God could and would heal me that night and I knew it beyond a shadow of a doubt. One of those who prayed for me had already walked my path and knew exactly how to pray. The relief was physical – it was like a tangible strength, full of light in my mind and heart. I came home and forgave from my heart those involved in my baby's death all those years ago. Then I surrendered her to Jesus and it was as if I was putting her in his arms and he took her. I know now that I am free and don't have to run any more; I don't have to see the emptiness peering round from behind the rush of busyness. Thank you, Father. Thank you, Jesus. Thank you, Holy Spirit." L.S.

"After a year of misery I had an instant healing for fibrositis. Later I felt it coming back and rebuked it in Jesus' name and the pain went away. This happened a few times, but I was sure that I could not accept anything less than complete healing. The pain was not able to get a hold, and I have been completely free of it for the past three years." F.J.

"In the service I ministered to a ten-year-old girl who had been afflicted with asthma since a baby, and who was progressively getting worse. As a result of the ministry she is now able to romp with other children, goes surfing and plays competition squash." J.R.

"My mother had a very deep ulcer on her leg, and her doctor made plans for a skin graft. I had the laying on of hands for her at the Cathedral, and on arriving home my mother mentioned a tingling and itching sensation at the time we had prayed. Within twenty-four hours pink flesh was appearing, and it was completely healed within four weeks." D.B.

"I have suffered from deep depression, but I have left this behind, and there has been no recurrence." H.D.

"In a progressive way over twelve years I have been healed of a serious thyroid condition." M.L.

"We have a friend who was crippled after a car accident seven years ago. She was reduced to lying on a couch, wore a surgical collar, had lost her singing voice, and could only take a very few steps with the use of sticks. Since coming to the need sharing service conducted by the Reverend Esdaile Barnes at Beverly Hills two years ago, she has been progressively healed. At the first service she lay on a lounge chair propped up on cushions. A couple of months later she could sit upright in the chair and a few months later again she had discarded her sticks and then her collar. She found she was able to go back to the church sitting in a comfortable chair. Then her voice returned and she could sing again and last Christmas sang a duet at a carol service. Before Christmas 1982 she was able to go to Sydney by train for the first time in seven years. She is beginning to drive again and is back to Sunday School teaching. Every month she has a further testimony and is praising God for continued healing." B.A.

"In October I contracted shingles. I had the laying on of hands and anointing with oil and after that there was very little pain and no irritation. In a very short time I was completely healed. The doctor said he had never seen shingles healed so quickly." P.V.

"My small son was covered with eczema from his head to his feet. Hospitalisation relieved the condition but on discharge it would return. It has been progressively healed by God in a miraculous way." S.

Question 3: If you have prayed for healing but you have not been healed, what effect has this had on your faith? Has God given other blessings?

"A man I work with, and his wife, both unbelievers at the time, came to the healing service with their baby son who was terminally ill and had been given only a few weeks to live. Both parents accepted Jesus as their Lord and Saviour that first night because of the loving support and consideration shown them by the members of the congregation. The baby died but the parents' faith has grown stronger and they have taken up local church membership." L.D.

"My faith continues to be in God – not my healing." M.P.

"My husband had cancer and for the six months before his death we both came to the healing service. During that time we both came to God and it was the best six months of our lives. Before he died my husband asked that part of his estate be given to the healing ministry as a mark of thanksgiving for the blessing received." Anon.

"We prayed and believed for healing by faith; the result was that we got to know God in a deeper and more meaningful way. Subsequently, when we came to realise that P. was not to be healed on earth, we knew God had a better plan and we were able to trust him for it. I believe we would not have been able to do that without the help and encouragement which we always received from you and from the healing ministry." C.D.

"After praying for a sick man with the laying on of hands and anointing there was a tremendous improvement in his attitude towards his family. Though he did not recover, he was no longer selfish and demanding during the rest of his illness." F.B.

Question 4: Is your general health better or not since you have been coming to the healing service?

"Yes, the encouragement and the instruction of the services provide a high motivation for me to be well." Anon.

"Yes!" B.C.

"My general health has improved tremendously, especially in this last year. I can pack much more into a day and enjoy it." W.L.

"My health has never been better and my mental attitude continues to be positive, whereas before it was negative to the point of being in a dungeon." R.L.

"My health, mentally and physically, is in perfect condition for the first time in thirty-eight years." S.N.

"Yes, by living according to God's laws, he has shown me how to avoid the causes or breeding grounds of so much of our sicknesses. I have learnt the truth of the saying from Proverbs, 'As a man thinks in his heart, so he is'." H.G.

"My general health is much better because I have peace of mind." R.B.

"Yes, all my family are in better health because we trust in the Lord now and don't worry in the same way." T.N.

Question 5: What help has the healing ministry been to you spiritually?

"The healing ministry brought a new dimension of faith for me. It brought Christianity to life in a real, practical and liveable way – not just 'pie in the sky' stuff. It brought the fullness of the Holy Spirit into my life." B.P.

"The meaning of wholeness and holiness has been opened to me. It has taught me to pray about social matters without my biased political opinions governing my prayers." L.M.

"I know him now not only as my Saviour but also as my close friend to whom I can talk about everything and thank him for everything. I pray the prayer of faith all the time and find it a great comfort." T.N.

"I have been re-grafted into the vine and the lost sheep has been found." H.D.

"It has brought excitement and expectancy into my prayer life as I have, for the first time, started praying the prayer of faith for myself and for others. It has resulted in increased praise and worship. God has brought me all the way to Australia (from England) in order to convince me intellectually about healing and then to heal me." V.C.

"The healing ministry has encouraged me in my theological studies and in the steady growth of the fruits of the Spirit." V.E.

"Of incalculable help! It has been the vehicle that has brought me back to Christ." W.J.

"Since coming to the healing service I have been baptised in my local church and have given my life to the Lord." R.D.

"I have received the Holy Spirit for service. I get an urge to smile at strangers as I walk down the street, just for the joy of seeing a worried face smile back." W.L.

"The healing ministry has given depth to my spiritual life whereas before, even though I had attended church services regularly all my life, it meant very little to me. Now I can honestly say it means everything to me." R.P.

Question 6: What effect has the healing ministry had on your work, your family, and your Sunday church activity?

"A new dimension has been added to my work as a clergyman and it rubs off to members of my congregation." B.E.

"Due to the healing ministry I pray for healing for my patients and God has given wonderful results. Our family is able to talk more openly about the Bible and I have made a commitment to attend worship regularly." H.D.

"I now drive to work at an orderly pace – no more rocket propulsion stuff. I am known as being different." C.B.

"The children have undoubtedly benefited from coming to the service and more because we know better how to pray for them. Answers to prayer are the rule!" B.R.

"It has been a wonderful talking point to introduce Christ to my work-mates." Anon.

"A business that involved me in questionable circumstances has been sold and I have started a new business which has been blessed by God through prayer." P.B.

"I wanted my Sunday activity to conform to what is done in the healing service. I did not express this in words but in attitudes. I now see I must be subject to my own rector and his wishes and support him in the way he wants to do things and pray for the congregation as a whole." A.B.

"The healing ministry has led us to associate with our parish church." L.T.

Any other comments?

"I am very confident to ask friends, especially in great need, to come to the services because I know their hearts will be opened to God and they will be blessed." P.V.

"I am in the process of learning to drive a bus so as to provide transport to the Healing Service and hope to include patients from Hornsby Hospital." H.D.

"Now I understand what trusting in the Lord is all about. I still fail again and again, but I know now that he is there to raise me up." R.P.

"The healing ministry has afforded a demonstration, which has been good for my soul, of the love of Jesus filling people and flowing out from them to many very needy people. Some of them are outcasts of society." M.B., B.S.

"This unique service has a sweetness about it which cannot really be put into words." N.T.

WHAT A MEDICAL PRACTITIONER CAN EXPECT

The healing ministry of the Christian church seeks to work in full association with the medical profession. They complement each other. Just as most people who draw on the healing ministry are also drawing on the medical resource, so too there are encouraging signs that medical and para-medical personnel are beginning to draw on the healing ministry resource. Here is the testimony of a medical practitioner (name supplied) who does that.

"This account involves my work as a senior medical officer during a nine-month term in a paediatric hospital. In-patient work rotated mainly in two areas: (1) general medical paediatrics and (2) the intensive care unit which mostly dealt with neonatal problems. This covered a wide range of the medical and surgical disorders associated with prematurity and complications of the newborn, with facilities including artificial ventilation for severe respiratory problems.

"During this time I endeavoured to pray individually for each baby or child every day while examining them (silently and unknown to the patient and those around). As time went on I began to feel that two things were happening: patients were recovering faster than when other people treated them; there were less complications of illness and treatment.

"These, of course, were only impressions and in no way were proven in a scientific manner, but gradually I became convinced that it was so. Other resident doctors would often talk about complications of illness in the general medical area. I was seeing very few complications, and although jealous at first of the fascinating medical experience I was missing, it led me to start thinking about the effect my prayer was having.

"It was in the intensive care unit that the effect was most noticeable, because of the rapidity of improvement and decline of many neonatal disorders. In I.C.U. I found that rarely did 'disasters' and deaths occur while I was on duty compared to their rather more common occurrence when others were on duty. Often I would find I had 'quiet days and nights' while the other resident doctors rotating twelve-hour shifts would have hectic days and nights with one or more serious complications occurring, e.g. pneumothorax, infection, intracranial or pulmonary haemorrhage. This seemed even more noticeable with one other resident (who was anti-Christian in many ways) where day after day the cycle went on – their twelve hours had at least one complication and during my twelve hours things would settle down, only to be repeated again the next twenty-four hours. In no way could I accept that our medical approach differed in any significant way.

"This, of course, is far from the double blind trial situation we have come to accept in medical research. (It would be interesting, perhaps, to try and design such a controlled trial.) However, it does seem reasonable to me that when we apply the principles of faith to our work in this way and ask the Lord to heal, he will answer our prayer and that we may very well be astounded at the results. I trust that this experience may encourage doctors to reach out to the Lord in believing prayer and so add a new dimension to the healing process." M.B., B.S.

PART 2

GUIDELINES FOR WORKERS IN THE HEALING MINISTRY

The second part of this book is particularly addressed to those who are ministering to troubled people. In our own healing ministry setting, that means every member of the congregation, clergymen and laymen alike. It is certainly addressed to clergy, because they have the role of leadership and ultimate responsibility. It is equally addressed to lay men and women, because in the early church everyone was involved in ministry, whether in witnessing or in laying on hands. Even the "tea-pourers" had an outreach followed by signs and wonders that was not secondary to that of the apostles in its effect.

It is also intended for those who are sick and are being ministered to – a very good way to get well is to help someone else get well! Our sickness/healing experience is precisely that which equips us to understand and assist others. At the same time, if you are new to helping in ministry, don't rush in. Watch and listen to those who are more experienced and learn from them.

These "guidelines for workers" give insights into ministry, an outline of counselling procedures, an introduction to deliverance, and a structure for one's daily prayer activity.

4

MINISTRY

IN ONE WAY and another, a good deal has been said about ministry already. In this chapter we refer, albeit briefly, to four areas of special concern to the worker in the healing ministry: teaching, Holy Spirit gifts, congregational unity and the ministry of all believers. We begin with teaching and refer to method and content.

Teaching

There are two ways of communicating the gospel. The first is to begin with what the Bible says; explaining it and relating it to what else is written in scripture so that a broad picture is gradually presented. The preacher may then go on and apply this to the circumstances in which people find themselves. This latter point is not always followed through; some of the most eminent expositors are quite content to explain the revelation in the Bible and leave it at that.

This approach might be thought of as being *deductive*, and would be, by far, the more usual way of preaching and teaching. Many excellent ministries stem from it, for which we can only be thankful to God.

Begin where people are

A second way is to begin where people are, so that their needs are seen to be understood and brought into focus. The need for healing is a simple illustration. The teacher then relates the relevant promise of God to the need. This means that sickness is covered by healing; fear by power, love and soundness of mind; sin by forgiveness, etc.

The point has been made already that the Holy Spirit makes both the immediate answer to prayer effective and also shows Christ to those concerned. This means that, as far as our witnessing about Christ is concerned, we may not *begin* by speaking about the Lord, but because of the dynamic involved, we will, with virtual certainty, do this *in the course* of the contact – and with many more people than if we try to present Christ straight away, but in a vacuum. It is like the circular wick in an old-fashioned kerosene stove; if you light it properly at one point, it isn't long before the flame spreads all the way round. If a person's need is met by the appropriate resource that God provides, the Holy Spirit will increasingly bring into focus and reality *all* the truth and blessing of our God. We play our part as we sensitively follow and complement the lead and ministry of the Spirit.

This approach might be referred to as being *inductive*. It is just as concerned with presenting God's word, but you *come to it*, rather than *go from it*. While these two methods do not exclude one another, a teacher tends to favour one rather than the other. The inductive method is what I follow in the healing ministry, and I suggest that workers in this field need to understand it and to learn to employ it effectively. There is nothing knew about it – it is the first principle in teaching: begin where people are.

This was the approach made by Jesus and Paul. So much of our Lord's teaching began at the point of need – the parables are an example. And which of St Paul's letters did not arise out of a problem being addressed? 1 Corinthians is an excellent example of one need after another being dealt with and developed into more extensive theology. *But* he stuck with the need or problem.

Far from the inductive approach lacking in the exposition of the scriptures, it is the principle in which so much of the New Testament scriptures were written!

Needs and answers

The content of my teaching at any one time comes from

my current needs and my current experience of drawing on the answers of God – the inductive approach. Because of this, I find that the people who listen tend to identify with what is said and feel that it has an application to them. This is not to say that my addresses are autobiographical; they are not, but the principle of need and answer that they seek to convey comes from my daily walk with God.

There are also the needs and answers of the many people to whom I am relating in a pastoral way. Because I am believing with them and for them, their needs and answers are part of me as well. I handle the experiences of other people in much more general terms, and am, of course, meticulous in preserving privacy. But even so, they make an important contribution to the relevance of my teaching. If I began to live in an ivory tower, and was no longer in the market place, my preaching would soon come to an end.

Complementing this, there is the need to be going further in one's understanding of God's word, so that the "precious and very great promises"[1] are seen ever more clearly in their range and detail. By the same token, there is the need to be going further in one's understanding of repentance, faith and obedience, whereby we appropriate God's gracious provision and have it in our real-life situation.

It is my considered view that a main reason why our healing service congregation has not only been maintained, but is still increasing, after nearly twenty-five years of active ministry, is because of the inductive method of teaching and ministering that has been described here.

Illustrations of the kind of subjects that are dealt with in our teaching ministry have already been given in the section, "Join a healing congregation" in Chapter 2.

Holy Spirit gifts

In the deep, person-to-person ministry that is required if the healing ministry is to be made effective, it is necessary to be able to draw on the relevant gift ministries that are provided by the Holy Spirit. To have, for example, the gifts of knowledge and discernment gives insight and authority that can be experienced in no other way. Holy Spirit gifts are not an optional extra; they are an essential prerequisite.

Every member of the body of Christ is expected to have some gift ministry. And when everyone in the congregation is putting his or her gift to work, we will see the range of ministries which God has for his church, and which are necessary to extend his kingdom. Then we will wonder how we ever did without them before we had them.

It is very simple to draw on a gift of the Spirit provided certain guidelines are understood and followed. The first requirement is to want to have a gift for ministry; we must earnestly desire to move into this dimension in the interests of helping other people. One then waits on God for his guidance as to what ministry he wills us to have. We can have this knowledge of God's will when we remember that he will use the natural aptitude with which he has already endowed us as an indicator of his further provision. He will also use the circumstances of our lives, so that what we have learned from our own permitted difficulties will be the area of help and ministry that we are to share with others.

While the gifts of the Spirit that are described in 1 Corinthians 12 and in other places in scripture are not to be modified in any way because they have been given by God in perpetuity (see Romans 11:29), I believe it is also true that, because we comfort others in the way we have been comforted, our gift ministry may not fall neatly into one category or another.

Once we have some sound idea about the direction in which we are to move, the next requirement is that we go forward in faith, and seek to exercise our gift according to the insights that we have at the present time. Let me illustrate this by referring to a woman of my acquaintance who has a remarkable gift of prophecy whereby she forth-tells the truth of God. When I asked her if she always had this gift, her reply was that at first she would just speak out what she believed God was saying to her. She added that as she looked back on that earlier time, she realised that to begin with it was only "my good ideas, with 'amen' on the end". But because she had faith *to make a beginning*, God honoured her faith, so that in a developing way the word she received was more and more a word from God.

I would say the same about myself. My own ministry did not "fall out of the blue", but has developed over the years in the way that has been described. In a word: know your gift(s) and develop it.

Supervision...

An essential requirement in the ministry of everyone, clergy and laity alike, is that it is subject to one's contemporaries. No one is entitled to say, "Thus says the Lord...", and for that to be the end of the matter. The word of God says, "Let two or three speak, and let the others weigh what is said."[2] This means that gift ministries need to receive corporate approval to have the validity that the Bible requires.

The natural and best way for this supervision to be exercised is in the simple and meaningful reality of congregational life. We support one another, guide one another, and, if need be, correct one another.

The minister's duty is to provide for the expression and use of these gift ministries within the activity of the congregation so that they are under group management. They don't have to be part of the main worship service; indeed, I believe they are more suited to small group activity. But if, for any reason, the minister does not see his way clear to do this, he has only himself to blame if his members develop characteristics which lack the balance and restraint that they would have had if he had instructed them and they one another. My own experience is that if one exercises a firm and fair hand, there are no problems in this matter, but rather "... the whole structure is joined together and grows into a holy temple in the Lord".[3]

... and growth

When all is said and done, the best way to grow in ministry is to react to the various circumstances that have been permitted in our life so that we depend on God more, and in consequence have his blessing by which we are enabled to mature further. The very difficulties that confront us have been permitted by God, so that we will come to faith in his many-sided provisions. Get that right, and every obstacle becomes an opportunity and every problem becomes a promise.

This matter of gift ministries is so important that it should be studied in depth. A book which sets out to do this, and which I recommend, is *You are My Sons* by Michael Harper (Hodder and Stoughton).

Congregational Unity

One of the essential requirements for workers in the healing ministry (and indeed in any other ministry) is that they have "the unity of the Spirit in the bond of peace".[4] This is expressed in the oneness that everyone in the group has with everyone else. In turn, this enables the Holy Spirit to be stirred up and to flow out as rivers of living water to provide the blessing which God alone can give. If, on the other hand, there is *disunity* in the congregation, the Spirit will be grieved, so there cannot be the blessing that is needed and is being prayed for.

Here is a story from our ministry to make the point. Some years ago we made a change in the way the laying on of hands was administered in our service; instead of being done by our leadership, lay and clerical, it was put into the hands of all regular members of the congregation. At the time, this caused a marked cleavage of opinion in our fellowship – those for and those against. I was in favour of the change; others saw difficulties and were strongly opposed. Nothing seemed able to bring us together, and our corporate ministry was being adversely affected, both in blessing received through prayer, and in the number of people attending the service.

With this division resting heavily on my mind, I went on vacation, and such was my burden during the time away that I was really brought to the "end of my tether". As a result I had one of my rare experiences of being spoken to in an articulate way by the Holy Spirit. The words that were formed in my mind were, "the holy community". That is what we should be like, but we were not. I felt deeply convicted about my own part in our loss of unity, and only wanted to make things right.

At the first healing service on my return, I prefaced my address from the pulpit by recounting what had happened while I was away, and then apologised to everyone for my part in the disagreement. This wasn't easy to do; but it was something I *had* to do. The response was immediate; in one way and another, everyone else started to express their regret as well, and before long our unity had been restored – and, as well, we received guidance from God that resolved the problem.

We have learned from our mistakes that if we are to have the blessing of the Holy Spirit in ministry, we must keep "short accounts" with God and with one another. Where there is strain in our relationships, we work at it positively until "the new has come".[5] We face the problem, discuss it, make restitution and pray. The example must come from the leadership, and everyone else must follow.

"The unity of the Spirit in the bond of peace" is absolutely vital if a ministry is to have sustained Holy Spirit blessing.

The ministry of all believers
A point we have made consistently is that every believer is to be a minister. By this, we most certainly do not mean that ever believer is just to do what is right in his own sight. He needs instruction and supervision – both from

the clergy and from his peer group.

The instruction, from my point of view, means that he is given a working knowledge of what is set out in this book. He is to be enabled to see the broad outline of what is being done and so be able to act intelligently in the area where his aptitude suggests he should concentrate. Instruction can be given through preaching, or in class, or in a one-to-one relationship. Obviously the clergy have to provide this resource and see that it is continued, though others may well be involved in the teaching.

Supervision is equally important and has to be constantly given. If something happens at our service to do with ministry that needs attention, I always attend to the matter myself and do it straight away. It may be that one of our leaders has reported something that was somewhat different from what it should be. I seek out the persons concerned and, in a courteous way, raise and discuss it with them. Their insights are important, as are mine, and together we work through the issues so that we come to a balanced conclusion. We never have the slightest difficulty in securing a positive response; everyone is only wanting the ministry to be as good as it can possibly be. It may well be that the leader concerned has attended to the matter, and that is just as good.

After every service, I go through what has happened carefully and note the faults and failures, and make them my special prayer projects for the following week. If we react in terms of the problems, they will be perpetuated; but if we react in terms of the answers, God is enabled to change things so that all is well.

Something else that needs to be said if a ministry of all believers is to become a reality, is that everyone concerned must want it and get behind it. This can by no means be assumed. So often the clergyman is used to being "a one man band", and so often the rank and file of a congregation are content to let that continue. It is comfortable, it is typical "churchianity" – but it is unproductive.

One thing is for sure: no one can be *argued* out of this position; to be able to rationalise the status quo is the easiest exercise in the book. The only thing that will change this situation is to have circumstances that will demand and require that the whole congregation be involved. I can only say that it has been an active healing ministry that has enabled the change to be made in my own ministry and congregation. I wonder if that is why our Lord told us to stretch out our hands to heal?

This hasn't always been comfortable. When people began to share in ministry, they also began to express opinions as to how the ministry should be exercised. More than this, where their view was different from mine, they were no longer willing to accept mine meekly just because I am a clergyman. And because we proceed only if we are unanimous in our conclusion, it requires a degree of listening to one another, and specially to the Lord, that is a constant spiritual discipline.

But it has made us a family of Christian brethren who are active in the Lord's work with signs following. There are aspects of it that we are still working through, but there is one thing about which we are all sure: the ministry of all believers is precious beyond words, and there isn't one of us who would go back to what it was like before.

5

COUNSELLING

THE PERSON SEEKING healing may need the important help that counselling provides. It will encourage
workers in the healing ministry to go further in providing
this resource, and those who need counselling to ask for it,
if its procedures are explained.

As with everything, balance is essential – and balance is
hard to come by. With Christian workers who are familiar
with counselling procedures, there is often too much
tendency to end up as social workers with "amen" on the
end. With Christian workers who are *un*familiar with
those procedures, there is too much tendency to present the
resource of Word and Sacrament in a vacuum without
relating it to the need and circumstance of the parishioner.

It isn't one or other, but both. Sound counselling
method needs to be allied to the gospel resource. Again,
this is hard to achieve, whether one is thinking in terms of
the worker or of what is in written form. What now
follows is intended to bring need and answer together as
they have been developed in this book, in terms of an
outline of counselling practice.

The first requirement is that the person in need must
want to be counselled. That means he has to take the
initiative in approaching the counsellor. If he wants to go
to his minister for this purpose, it may be well to suggest
that on the way out of church, when the minister is trying
to relate to other members of the congregation as well, is
not the best time to ask him. As far as the minister himself
is concerned, he should not allow himself to be
monopolised in this way (it happens a lot), so that others

pass by without receiving the greeting they would otherwise be given. If this occurs, the enquirer should be asked to wait for a short time until the matter can be discussed.

The counsellor (whatever the circumstances) also needs to be sensitive to the possibility that the person making the approach may have had to pluck up courage to come forward and could easily be put off by a vague assurance that he will be seen some time. There is nothing wrong in making a later time if that is necessary; the important thing is to make a definite arrangement that is mutually convenient, so that the enquirer goes away knowing when he is to come for the interview.

Perhaps a word might also be said about the physical arrangements for this kind of meeting. The important thing is that the person being counselled is made to feel at ease; the room should be tidy, the chairs comfortable but not too comfortable, the telephone switched off, an "engaged" sign placed on the door, and adequate time given for the conversation. An hour is ample; if more time is required, another interview can be arranged. It is not a good arrangement to speak over a desk, and the chairs should be slightly angled to each other, so that the two people can either look at one another or look away in an easy and natural manner.

Acceptance

Of great importance is the acceptance that the counsellor gives to those he counsels. He, or she, must have a compassionate interest in helping troubled people. If the counsellor ever becomes case-hardened, it is time to look for a less demanding sphere of work. That acceptance will not be properly given if he is trying to see more people than he has time available for, or emotional energy to cope with. It is better to say "no" to someone in need if, for this or any other reason, he will not be adequately helped and cared for. The appropriate response in these circumstances is to direct the enquirer to someone else who may be able to assist, and to refer him in a proper way.

The acceptance the counsellor shows is what he feels within himself, and which comes out in his manner and ministry. It is something that will continue on from interview to interview, so that the person being counselled will find his confidence increasing as time goes by.

This can be time-consuming business. I remember once seeing someone and feeling that what he said about himself did not adequately explain the degree of emotional disturbance he had. But he was so insecure, that if I had pressed the matter, he would have felt threatened, and very likely the counselling relationship would have come to an end. I continued to show acceptance in interview after interview, until some eighteen months after we had begun to meet, he said to me one day, "Canon Glennon, I am going to tell you what the real trouble is." Then he told me things about which he was highly sensitive, and which explained the symptoms he had. After this he began to get well, and he is now completely restored and living a normal life. The psychiatric prognosis at that earlier time had been "very poor indeed". It is a good illustration, though somewhat extreme as to the time taken, of the role of acceptance and of the blessing that comes from it.

Listening

The next requirement is that of listening. Let me introduce this with a story. A clergyman once contacted me and asked whether he could bring one of his parishioners to me for counselling, and whether he could also sit in on the interview. This was agreeable to me, provided that it was all right with the parishioner. For some reason the interview did not go well, and when the woman had departed I said, "Nicholas, I'm sorry the interview was not very productive of counselling procedures." He looked at me with marked surprise and said, "But it was. You *listened* to her! If that had been me, I would have hoed in with good advice."

You can always tell the trained counsellor; he listens to the person in need. You can always tell the untrained counsellor; he "hoes in with good advice".

There are a number of reasons why the counsellor listens. As well as his listening being a sign of his concern, it is necessary, if he is to give help in a meaningful way, for the problem to be spelt out, and in enough detail to give depth of understanding. He can assist in this by showing an interest in, and an understanding of what is said, and by avoiding anything that would cut across the point and flow of the story.

As important as the story, indeed more so, are the feelings that accompany it and the need for them to be expressed as well. For example, if in relating some incident, distress is shown in the tone of voice, or by crying, or in "body language", the appropriate response is something like, "This experience must be very upsetting for you." This may well lead to a further release of feeling, which the counsellor should allow to happen without showing embarrassment. It is the feeling that accompanies the story that is the "hurt", and the fact that it is coming out in this way shows that, so far, it has been "buried".

To begin with, the person being counselled will tend to speak about things that are on the surface and socially acceptable. It will only be as confidence grows that he will be able and willing to talk about the deeper and more significant things. At the same time, the counsellor, if he is experienced and sensitive, can do much to enable the significant material to be brought out. As the story progresses, the occasional appropriate question is asked that begins to guide things along, so that the counsellee is both "getting it off his chest" and giving the kind of information that will enable the problem to be solved.

Understanding

The counsellor is listening so that he can understand how this person is functioning; to discern his strengths and weaknesses, and to see something of the underlying factors and how they combine to produce the problem the person presents.

With this in mind, let me say that the approach I usually follow to bring out these underlying factors is to ask how long the problem has existed. The next question is what were the circumstances that applied at that earlier time, or in the period up to the two years before that. The answers you get depend on the questions you ask, and the questions you ask depend on what you are looking for, and what you are looking for depends on your understanding and experience of how problems evolve and develop. The principle in the story of Joyce Hansen, who had a long-standing physical ailment co-extensive with her grudge against her sister-in-law, can be repeated over and over again, though I would add one thing: it isn't always as simple as that – problems can be complex and multi-factored.

This is the kind of understanding that I am looking for – the kind of buried hurt that needs to be brought to the surface, the more so because the counsellee often doesn't have this understanding, and doesn't see its significance as far as the present situation is concerned. I have already said that I spend a considerable time in a counselling interview helping the person concerned to have this understanding, because that in itself will relieve tension and lessen confusion: it enables him to see his real problem and face up to it in a constructive and remedial way. I am not saying that "the buried hurt syndrome" always applies, but I believe it does so much more than is commonly realised. Where it can be reasonably seen to apply, these insights need to be drawn on if healing is to be experienced in depth and permanence.

Sometimes the sick person doesn't want to see things in these terms because to do so is too threatening, and he will defend himself in various ways. That must be respected. The counsellor can only go as far and as fast as the counsellee is able and willing to respond. The counsellee may well be able to go further at a later time, as his confidence grows.

Ministering

We now come to the ministry that is relevant to the understanding we now have. There are three elements to this. The first is to know the appropriate resource that God has promised, and then to explain its relevance. For example, and using the case study illustrations that have already been referred to, the answer to fear is the power, love and soundness of mind that God has made available. The answer to resentment is forgiveness. The answer to a burden is to cast it on the Lord. The answer to buried hurt is inner healing. The answer to loneliness is the companionship that Christ offers. And the answer to someone who is without God in his life is the salvation that comes from the Lord Jesus and his work on the cross.

This can be multiplied almost endlessly; if we concerned ourselves with the promises of God all our life, there would be still more waiting to be fully understood and drawn on. To this end we must always remain prayerful students of the Bible, because we are entirely dependent on the scriptures as being the place where the promises are found.

The second element in ministry is always to say to the one being counselled that he has to switch over from affirming the problem to affirming the answer. This has been set out clearly in the first chapter, and will repay further reading. It cannot be repeated too often that to react in terms of the initial difficulty will only perpetuate it. It is vital that one reacts by accepting and affirming the appropriate answer from God. As we are so wedded to the problem, the point will need continued reinforcement by the counsellor and continued perseverance by the person being helped before the needful change is experienced in the degree that is required.

Sometimes I put it like this. Because our affirmation of the difficulty has been going on for so long, it is as though the ship of our life is going full speed astern. Even when our reactions are in terms of the answer of God, or, to continue our simile, the engines have been put "full ahead", it will take time for the backward movement of the vessel to be arrested. The ship will slowly come to a stop and remain motionless briefly before it begins to move ahead, very slowly at first, then more quickly. This is a good simile, because it describes accurately what happens, as well as giving understanding to the person whose ship it is, so that he will continue to react positively and appropriately when he doesn't see the full answer straight away.

It has to be said that we only really get this right *when we have to*. Indeed, I would go further and say that we only ever exercise faith to the point where we do not doubt in our heart, when we have to – yet we choose to. We all know people who continue with their difficulties because they don't have to change. We all know people (perhaps we have been in that position ourselves) who have accepted the answer to their problem because they were in a crisis situation and had no alternative but to do so. The alcoholic is a well-known illustration, but there are many others that are more ordinary and closer to home. Sometimes the counsellor has to create a crisis, so that the person being helped is brought to see that this is what he has to do if his life is to be changed for good.

Having faith together

The third factor in relevant ministry is exercising faith with and for the person in need. Of course, to change over from affirming the problem to affirming the answer is faith-in-action. Reaching that point will be much helped by prayer, when these things are put into the kind of terminology that we use for conversion.

When I come to this point in an interview, I say to my visitor that he had faith to come, and I am now going to add my faith to his so that we are believing together. The more faith he has, the easier it is for my faith to help him;

the less faith he has, the more difficult. But no one ever leaves the healing ministry in St Andrew's Cathedral having been told that he hasn't enough faith, because if he has faith to come, the reference in James 5:14, 15 makes it clear that it is then the responsibility of the church to pray over him. And that is what I am doing for him and with him at this point in the interview.

Usually I go further and say that I accept faith responsibility for him. This is just taking belief for others to its logical conclusion. It is what we do every time in infant baptism. The faith of the parents and godparents so avails for the child that it is affirmed that he is now "regenerate and grafted into the body of Christ's Church".[1] In other words, I am allowing the person in need to be wholly dependent on me for the exercise of prayer, at least at this time.

This places great demands on me. I have to discipline my mind and spirit to have faith for those I counsel, so that as a result God is enabled to bless them (see Mark 2:3, 5, 11). At an earlier time, I spent many years trying to help troubled people to believe for themselves; and I got a short way in a long time. It is understandable; it is difficult to have faith which does not doubt when you have the pain and the anxiety. There have been infinitely better results since I have been standing in the breach and believing for such people (and with them). The explanation is not far to seek; the outsider's faith is relatively objective, whereas faith for oneself is subjective. Experience has also shown that when prayer is made for someone in this way, he is brought to faith himself in a quite remarkable way. So all needs are being met.

I pray something like this: "Thank you, Father, for the faith your servant has in coming here today and for the understanding you have given as we have talked together. We praise you for your promise of healing revealed in the scriptures, and we now accept that healing for him according to his need. We accept it as we accept Christ for salvation; we accept it so it is what we have decided and what we now affirm. We praise you by faith that your blessing is now flowing to him, and by your grace we continue to affirm the answer in a present-tense kind of way. Thank you, Father, for what you are doing now, through Christ our Lord, Amen.''

As a general rule, I do not see people for counselling unless they are coming to the healing service and have attended at least two or three times. It is in their interest to know something of how the healing ministry functions, because – and this is a very important point – the service is our therapeutic activity. It is where the teaching takes place. It is where the corporate support and faith are being expressed. It is where the person is beginning to make his response to the promise of God. Otherwise it can be hard work beginning "from cold", and the end result is never as good as when the counsellee has something of what happens at the service "under his belt".

One-to-one ministry

In my view, a main reason why our ministry has been effective and acceptable over the years, with a very wide variety of people and circumstances, is our emphasis on a one-to-one relationship, not only in counselling, but in everything. We have never dealt with people in the mass. Our approach is time-consuming and draining, but it is necessary and productive and used by God. There are no short cuts.

There is one thing more. Although I allow people to be completely dependent on me to begin with so that they are receiving a kind of faith transfusion, this is only designed to help them get on their own faith feet. Usually I do not see people more than three or four times, and by then they are learning to believe for themselves. Again, balance is the important thing. It is counter-productive for people to become too dependent on the counsellor if this goes on past a certain point. Some people need a more on-going contact, and we all need continuing support in one form or another; but sooner or later, there is no substitute for the individual's own relationship with God and his own exercise of faith in drawing on the blessings of God.

* * *

I have never ceased to be grateful for the social-work training that was given me in my earlier years. It taught me to understand people and to relate to them in an informed way. The insights and discipline of counselling method have been a great stand-by and are indispensable in helping troubled people.

When my former Archbishop (the late Dr H.W.K. Mowll) asked me to do this course at the University of Sydney, I could not have been more indifferent. But when I got into it and saw something of its contribution to thought and action, I remember exclaiming, "Why didn't they teach me this in theological college?" If the theological graduate is not also taught to understand the people to whom he ministers, his message will often be as seed sown by the wayside. But if he really knows the needs people have and relates his teaching to them, his message will be much more likely to fall on good ground and bring forth much fruit.

6

DELIVERANCE

The story of "Sandy" Thompson

"SANDY" THOMPSON WAS a big man, such as you would expect to see playing first-grade football; it made his story all the more unusual and unexpected. Perhaps this was why he found it difficult to come to the point about his problem. Finally he told me that when he was asleep at night he felt someone was sitting on his chest and trying to suffocate him. He would fight back, trying to gulp in air, and would finally wake up shouting – even screaming with fear. This, of course, was highly distressing to both himself and his wife, as well as to their small son who, as a result, was showing signs of emotional disturbance. No amount of thinking it through and talking it out had made any difference; he was in the grip of something he could not control. The contrast between his strong frame and tormented face made the story all the more poignant and help more urgent.

He ended his story by looking at me very directly and saying, "I can't carry on; is there anything you can do to help me?"

Of myself there was nothing I could say or do. I said a prayer silently that a Salvationist had taught me, "Holy Spirit, over to you."

"Would you like to tell me how long things have been like this?' I asked him. He furrowed his brow and said, in a hesitant way, "As far as I can remember . . it began when I was about sixteen."

"Did anything happen at that point in your life which might explain why things began to go wrong?"

"I am not sure," he replied, "but I will tell you what happened about that time. An aunt had died, and my brother hypnotised me and made me get in touch with the spirit of our dead aunt. Something happened so that we thought a reply had been given. My brother became afraid and pulled out, but I wanted to continue and would go secretly to her grave and try and talk with her spirit. It was a kind of conversation, if you know what I mean. It was from this time that things started to go wrong; not much to begin with, but it gradually became worse. Now I am afraid to go to bed at night. I know what will happen."

"Well, at least I can tell you what your trouble is all about," I replied. "I don't doubt that something happened when you tried to communicate with your deceased aunt. But that is a very dangerous thing to do and is expressly forbidden in scripture. You see, there are *two* spirit forces in the world; there are the things of God – Father, Son and Holy Spirit – and there is the kingdom of Satan as well. He doesn't always come with horns and tail, but comes, the Bible says, as an angel of light and would deceive, if it were possible, even the elect of God.

"I don't say that every time someone does something wrong and foolish such as you have described, they will have a bad experience. But when things go wrong – and they have gone wrong for sure as far as you are concerned – it is because, in almost every case, the person concerned has been dabbling in the occult, of which this is a very well-known example. I cannot avoid the conclusion that because you opened yourself to that kind of activity, an unclean spirit has come into you and is the cause of your trouble."

He had no difficulty in accepting my explanation, pleading that what he had done had been done in ignorance. When we had worked through this, I went on to explain how Christ came to destroy the works of Satan, and that this power and freedom were still available today when we prayed in faith.

At this he shook his head, saying, "I haven't got any

faith. I am too sick with fear to help myself."

I smiled. "Yes, you have; you had faith to come, and I am going to add my faith to yours for God's blessing. You can leave it to me; I am going to believe for you and with you." I then prayed for him:

"In the name of the Father, and of the Son and of the Holy Spirit, Amen. Father, in invoking the name and the power of the Trinity I am believing for protection for myself and everyone else.

"In the name of Jesus Christ, I now bind the strong man who is oppressing your servant, and thereby believe that the spirit force that is in him or around him is being rendered powerless.

"In the name of Christ I now loose the strong man, bound and powerless, from this man. We rejoice that that which is loosed on earth is loosed in heaven; because we act on earth in Christ's name, God acts so that we draw on his power and ministry now.

"I now direct that this spirit force goes to the place that God has prepared for it, and remain there never to return.

"Father, in its place I believe your servant is being filled with all the fullness of God and protected with the armour you provide, that he may be able to stand against the evil one.

"I accept this blessing like we accept Christ for salvation. Thank you, Father, by faith in Jesus' Name, Amen."

I arranged for my visitor to come to see me again so that the matter could be followed through. But it has to be said that when he came things hadn't changed much for the better. I disciplined my prayer thinking to avoid having the reaction that it wasn't working, and instead affirmed, "Father, I am believing this by faith, and by faith I praise your name for answered prayer."

When "Sandy" came the next time the improvement was more obvious. He came to see me six times in all, and there was meaningful growth and change for the better as time went by. The horrific experiences at night began to decline in severity and happened less frequently, until finally they didn't return at all. Now the big man was smiling and feeling that life was worth living again and that God was good. He was already a professing Christian, and what had happened did much to confirm his faith and make God real to him at the present time.

Later on something else happened that made a wonderful postscript. His wife, it so happened, was a Moslem, and she was so impressed with the change in her husband's condition through discernment and prayer that, of her own volition, she went to the rector of the parish where they lived and asked to be prepared for Christian baptism. Those who know something of how difficult it is for a Moslem to be converted to Christianity will appreciate the strength and reality of this testimony.

Ever since then, I have had the view that if Christian missions among Moslem people were more effective in exercising a healing and deliverance ministry, the person of Jesus would more easily be seen to be the Son of God and the Saviour of the world.

If what has been said seems bizarre, I can only say that that is one of the characteristics of this phenomenon, both now and in Bible times. What could be more bizarre than the story in Mark Chapter 5, of the man who was mad because he was indwelt by many unclean spirits which, after a verbal exchange with Christ, left at his command to enter a herd of pigs, who then ran over a cliff to their destruction? We have to be careful that we do not venerate an account of something that happened two thousand years ago, while remaining full of reasons (*sic*) why it doesn't happen like that today.

In a way that has not been sought, I have had a low-key deliverance ministry over the years of my involvement in the healing ministry. I can give numerous case studies that would illustrate what it is like in practice. The one given was chosen because it brings into focus a good deal of the dynamic that is involved, both in discernment and in remedial prayer.

There is no need to say to anyone who reads the New Testament that this kind of ministry was recognised and practised by our Lord in a way that leaves no room for misunderstanding. Not only was Satan a real person – so too were his ministering spirits. They inhabited people; they were destructive in operation; they could speak and act with intelligence as well as respond to direction.

Discernment and diagnosis

The means by which we determine whether or not a problem is caused by this direct work of Satan is what the Bible refers to in 1 Corinthians 12 as the "discernment of spirits". This means that one can distinguish between the work of the Holy Spirit and that of the unclean spirits. Complementing this, there are certain patterns of activity that will enable one to recognise this problem when it is there.

But there can be other possible explanations that need to be "checked out". I have had people referred to me because it was believed that they were oppressed in this way, only to find that their degree of disturbance was caused by emotional factors that had nothing whatever to do with unclean spirits. It would only add to their disturbance to foist on to them a deliverance explanation that did not apply, as well as leaving the real problem untouched.* The reverse also applies. Some people in need of this ministry are being seen by clergy and doctors who, because they do not understand this spiritual dimension, are giving a wrong diagnosis and treatment, as well as leaving the real cause unchanged.

Beware of the occult

By far the most common circumstance that leads to

---

*Part of the treatment of what is called "the possession syndrome" by those psychiatrists who include this in their medical practice, is first to examine the patient for a more orthodox explanation of his problem. Only if his difficulty lies outisde these parameters is "the possession syndrome" considered.

oppression or possession is involvement in the occult, take what form it may. As far as my experience goes, I have no hesitation in saying that in nine cases out of ten this is the basic cause. Ouija boards, tarot cards, astrology and horoscopes, seances, spiritism, black magic, etc., all expose the participant to spirit forces that only come from Satan. As we have already said, they may seem innocent and harmless to begin with. Involvement does not always lead to a bad experience, but where there *is* a bad experience, this is where it has come from.

It follows that anything like this should be strictly avoided by everybody, Christian and non-Christian alike. More than this, the Christian needs to learn to protect himself, because part of the story is that these spirit forces can leave the person in whom they are dwelling and move to another host. For example, a person ministering to someone who has this difficulty can find that, as a result of his prayer in the name of Jesus, the unclean spirit leaves the person concerned but enters the one who is doing the praying.

This has happened to me at an earlier time. I remember praying for a young woman who was depressed and confused following occult involvement and who was wonderfully released following the prayer. But I found myself in black despair. For some days I didn't understand what had happened, but when I thought back to when my distress began I realised that it was at the time of my ministry with the girl. Then I asked one of my prayer partners to pray for my own deliverance and the spirit of heaviness left me.

There is no need for the counsellor to be fearful about this. We protect ourselves by knowing that Christ has won the victory over Satan and has provided "the shield of faith with which you can quench all the flaming darts of the evil one" (Ephesians 6:16) and by drawing on that protection by faith, i.e. we accept the protection and affirm it in praise.

Principles of deliverance

Here is the procedure to be followed in a prayer for deliverance, together with some comments:

The first requirement has already been referred to: the need for protection for those who are ministering.

The next is for the person being delivered to confess his occult involvement/contact with spirits, whether that has happened deliberately or through ignorance. As well as confession being an instruction in scripture, it gives an awareness of the "wrong-ness" of the matter, and relates the sin to the *forgiving* power of Christ.

Complementing this, there is need for an act of renunciation, whereby the person concerned shows his willingness to turn from his occult/spirit involvement (with the help of God), and not return to the former ways. This enables him to draw on the *cleansing* power of Christ.

The spirit forces are then rendered powerless by binding them. "No one can enter a strong man's house . . . unless he first binds the strong man."[1] When this is done with believing prayer, it will have the effect of preventing any manifestation that otherwise can be bizarre and frightening.

Jesus said, "Whatever you loose on earth shall be loosed in heaven."[2] God gives us power for ministry, and we need to know what that power is and how to draw on it. The bound spirits are now separated or "loosed" from the host or wherever else they have been. It may help to visualise the person or place being cleansed by the sanctifying power of the Holy Spirit.

The next requirement is to direct the spirits to go to the place that God has prepared for them, and not to return and enter into anyone else. Our Lord specifically warned that this could happen.[3] I well remember at an earlier time (and before I had learned this lesson the hard way), that I had exercised a ministry of deliverance with a missionary who had been working in Papua New Guinea, where there is much animistic worship (which is another potent source of this kind of problem), as a result of which she had become oppressed by these spirit forces. She had been forced to return from the mission field because of this and had been referred by her mission society to a Christian psychiatrist. But because he did not understand this dimension, he had not been able to help her.

The day after my ministry to her, a medical student, who had been forced to discontinue his course because of emotional stress, came for counselling. When I prayed with him for God's blessing in an ordinary, straightforward way, to my great surprise and concern he began to writhe and became very, very distressed. I had seen this phenomenon before, and recognised it as something that can happen when spirit forces come into someone. Then I prayed for him silently, using the insights of deliverance, until he regained his composure and was none the worse for his experience. My opinion is that the spirit force that had been cast out from the woman had waited around and had entered this unprotected man, whose resistance had been lowered because of illness.

The positive side of this ministry is to believe that the person or place is being filled with the things that belong to the one true God. For example, our body is intended to be a temple of the Holy Spirit, and we are to be filled with the Spirit.[4]

There is also need for protection from further inroads by Satanic spirits. This is the whole purpose of the armour of God "with which you can quench all the flaming darts of the evil one".[5] This protection is drawn on by knowing it is available and believing for it in the same way that the other provisions of God are believed for.

Not least, there is the need for the person concerned to continue to draw on the means of grace whereby we are fed and upbuilt with God's sustaining strength received through Word and Sacrament. Where possible, the delivered person should be linked to a small prayer/support/study group for this ongoing ministry.

Much more can be said about this ministry. I trust that enough has been written to indicate something of its need and practice. I would add two things more: this is not a ministry for the novice; and the truth of these matters is the mean between two extremes: one extreme is to debunk this dimension, and the other is to see demons in every shadow.

Principal Detmar Scheunemann, of the Indonesian Bible Institute, gave an address on this subject at the Billy Graham sponsored International Congress on World Evangelisation in Lausanne in 1974, in which he said, "The tremendous need for a deliverance ministry is evident. It will still increase as the demonic powers are building up for the reign of the antichrist. Therefore a deliverance ministry should be an integrated part of end-time evangelism."[6]

The need for discernment and deliverance is certainly on the increase, and the worker in the healing ministry will, sooner or later, be confronted with it. What has been written will enable him to respond intelligently and effectively and, not least, will prompt him to call for more experienced advice and help when that is necessary.

7

PRAYER

IT HARDLY NEEDS to be said that every Christian worker should have a time every day for prayer and the reading of God's word. In this way we are built up in our understanding of what has been revealed to us in the Bible, and increased in the reality of the Holy Spirit within us.

For some, this will take a set form as in liturgical worship; and for others it will be extemporary. There will be those who prefer to have this time on their own in the privacy of their room, and there will be those who seek to do so in the company of others. These options do not exclude one another, but are complementary, so that each should be drawn on when need and opportunity combine. Our purpose is to set out some of the things to be considered when the individual is on his own and his prayer is informal. At the same time, a good deal of what is said will apply irrespective of what form of prayer is used.

Start the day right

Our first action every morning should be to "set" ourselves in relationship with God by affirming our position in Christ. Usually I say, "In the name of the Father and of the Son and of the Holy Spirit," and follow that with a time of praise for the night past and the day ahead.

Some will appreciate the more elaborate prayer used by the Reverend Terry Fullam, the Rector of St Paul's Episcopal Church in Darien:

I take God the Father to be my Lord,
I take God the Son to be my Saviour,
I take God the Holy Spirit to be my Sanctifier,
I take the word of God to be the rule of my life,
I take the people of God to be my people.
And now I commit myself – mind, body and spirit,
to my Lord and Saviour Jesus Christ;
and I do this freely, fully and for ever.
In the name of the Father, and of the Son, and of the
    Holy Spirit.

One reason for doing this is that, as his children by
adoption and grace, it is our humble duty to honour our
heavenly Father on waking, and confess our continuing
dependence on him for his personal and providential care.
Another, and more pragmatic, reason is that our needs are
not going to wait for our "Quiet Time", especially if there
is any kind of delay before it begins. How the day will turn
out depends so much on how we begin it. If, from our
earliest waking moments, we are affirming God's presence
and blessing, we will find that it will be relatively easy to
continue like this, and for our prayer time, when we have
it, to be an uplifting experience. But, on the other hand, if
we allow our needs to sweep over us so that we become
problem-orientated, we will find it difficult to change
course later during the day.

Structure and content

Let us now come to the Quiet Time itself. Don't be rigid
in thinking that you have to work this through in a certain
way. Of course, it may be a help to follow someone else's
guidelines to begin with, but sooner or later we have to do
what is right as far as *we* are concerned, which means that
we need to listen to God and have his guidance. This will
not come all at once, but will be a growth experience, that
we will learn by trial and error. In a word: we need to find
what suits us best.

With most people it helps to have the Quiet Time in the

same place and at the same time each day. This assists in promoting regularity and enables good prayer habits to be formed.

Many would want to begin with a reading from scripture (certainly the reading of God's word is an integral part of our time with God, but when and where this takes place is for the individual to decide). What is important with Bible reading, is that it is structured in a way that the Bible Reading Fellowship or Scripture Union or the Church Lectionary provides, so that the scriptures are read and understood in an ordered and progressive way. Nothing is more unrewarding to serious Bible study than just to "dip in" to the Bible as fancy chooses. After the reading, its contents should be turned into prayer, whereby we thank God for what has been revealed in his word and develop our prayer in any way that the reading may suggest.

As far as I am concerned, from there I go to what is otherwise uppermost in my mind and pray about it, whether it be to do with myself or someone else. To have a need so that there is only God to depend on, sweeps one into the presence of God with immediate and continued intercession. Not least, it provides concentration in prayer, which can be a problem on some occasions.

A major part of my own prayer time is spent praising God for answers to prayer that have been received recently – and, perhaps especially, praising God for answers to prayers that are being affirmed by faith. We have already referred to this as "soaking prayer".

Then I come to the point where I am moved to exercise faith in a positive way for matters in which, up till then, I have been affirming the difficulty. (The problems are to bring us to the promises – do you remember?) This is where I accept the answer and begin to affirm it. Other matters will come to mind in which I have already accepted God's provision, but need to confirm my acceptance and my faith affirmation, and correct any tendency I may have to be ambivalent, whereby I am accepting both the answer and the problem together.

It has been said already that it is helpful in this connection to believe and affirm that the answers are coming in a present-tense kind of way. I strictly avoid letting the word "will" come into my prayer, because "will" never comes. Jesus said we are to believe that we "have received" these things – by faith.

At this point, we might answer the question: should we *ask* more than once? The answer will be seen, when the matter of "asking" in prayer is put in the wider context of "believing" in prayer. We ask so that we might then believe. All I can say is that my own practice is to ask *once* and believe in a *continuing* way.

The matter of resentment and the need for forgiveness is also something that needs to be considered in the setting of one's personal prayer time. When I finally come to the point of kneeling down and praying through a matter like this, I have always, and without exception, come to the point of being convicted by the Holy Spirit of my own failures in the matter and the need for my own repentance. In other words, the Holy Spirit has shown me the beam in my own eye, whereas before I was convinced about the mote in someone else's eye. This leads to confession and restitution and a new way of thinking and praying about the matter. And when that happens, a whole new "ball game" comes into being.

Another use of one's Quiet Time is preparation for ministry; which means that I am concerned with the re-charging of my spiritual batteries. This requires prepara-tion, as shown in repentance, confession, forgiveness and cleansing. Then I concentrate on being filled with the Spirit, so that I believe for that in faith and praise. Complementing this, there is the need to believe for all details of the ministry that is to be exercised, including, of course, the people who will be there.

Continue in prayer...

When I have worked through the content of my time of

prayer, which ideally should take about an hour, my next prayer task is to make this the on-going way I am thinking and reacting and affirming. Unless the Quiet Time is translated into on-going action, it doesn't serve the purpose it should. "Faith apart from works is dead."[1] As far as possible, I make it the way my mind is "ticking over" during the rest of the day.

As well as the morning Quiet Time, I have a prayer time at *midday*, when I bring into focus more briefly the affirmations of my earlier prayers, as well as what may have come up during the morning's activities. Since we have had the Hour of Prayer at the Cathedral at 12 noon, this has become my midday time of prayer. Perhaps I might add, at this point, that for some time I felt I couldn't spare the time for an hour of prayer in the middle of the day, and tended to think of the other work that was waiting to be done. But as time has gone by, and I have seen the blessings that have come from the prayer meeting, I realise that it isn't so much a question of whether I can afford the time, but rather, whether I can afford *not* to use the time in this way?

There is one thing more I would like to mention in general terms about one's Quiet Time, and it is this: sometimes the question is asked, "Can we be 'on top' all the time?" My personal reply is that I am not "on top" all the time, but I believe we can come to that point every day, if the principles in this book are followed through. I certainly make that my aim, and have no hesitation in saying that it is attainable – and that we should move towards it more and more.

... and watch in the same with thanksgiving

At the *end of the day* I concentrate on thanksgiving. I look back on the day's activities and wait on the Holy Spirit to reveal to me the blessings he has given. When something is shown me of this kind, I praise God. Then the Spirit will show me something else that is positive, and, again, I will return thanks. I do not concern myself with what might remain to be made right or with things that have gone wrong, but give myself over to being thankful for what there is to be thankful for.

To me, one of the poignant episodes in our Lord's ministry was that of the ten lepers who were healed, and only one returned to give thanks. Our Lord's rebuke, "Where are the nine?", must be something that often applies to us as we take his blessings for granted and do not take the trouble to acknowledge them. It isn't altogether wide of the mark to say that a saint is someone who returns thanks to God. I seek to retire for the night on this note of praise.

Seek God for himself

If it were possible to say everything about prayer, it would still be true that the most meaningful prayer we can make is to seek God for himself, and to ask nothing, except to know that we do his will. This is what is meant when Jesus said, "Seek first his kingdom and his righteousness."[2]

If you are praying for healing and despite what you have done there isn't an answer in those terms, then lay your need on the altar, as Abraham did Isaac, *and seek God for himself*. This means that you are no longer seeking healing or any other needful blessing, but that you are content to be filled with all the fullness of God, Father, Son and Holy Spirit.

At an earlier time and for a time, we exercised the healing ministry on those lines. That is, we came to the point of looking past the need for healing, and were content for God to impart more of himself to us. And that is what he did; it was experience of unparalleled growth in Godliness. We also experienced much healing being added to us as our heavenly Father was pleased to meet our earthly needs as well.

I am not saying that it is easy to do this, but there is nothing worth while that is easy. We get these things right when we have to - yet we choose to. But when we do, we find that God is no man's debtor.

Guidelines for workers

I would emphasise that what has been presented in this part of the book is to be complemented by the pastoral guidelines in Part 1. Even so, what one can set out helps the worker only up to a certain point. In the long run, he/she has to draw on help from many sources and integrate it into a pattern that is meaningful and effective for him or her. And even then – that is no substitute for experience.

Having said that, what has been set out is a good deal of what I (and we) have found to be relevant and significant as far as our ministry is concerned, and our hope and prayer are that others will find it to be of assistance to them as well.

* * *

How can I find healing?

These words express the need, the question, and the search of so many people, Christian and non-Christian alike. It would be presumptuous to affect to provide the answer in one short volume, or that any one person can provide the answer however much were written. But what has been written here is intended to refer the person in need to the Lord Jesus Christ, of whom it was said he went about "healing every disease and every infirmity among the people",[3] and who commissioned his followers, both then and now, "to preach . . . and to heal".[4] However much the church has failed in fulfilling that responsibility, doesn't lessen the fact that the resource God provides is "irrevocable",[5] and is therefore available in our own day and in our own circumstances.

What has been set out is intended to be a balanced presentation of what the New Testament says in this connection: problems are to bring us to the promises of God. We draw on the promises by repentance, faith and obedience. In this we have a personal responsibility, as do the other believers with whom we have fellowship. Answer to prayer can be immediate or gradual, and the factors involved need to be understood and examined. And, not least, there is a limitation to healing when the greater reality of eternity is also taken into account.

More important than temporal healing is the eternal healing of our relationship with God and which Christ alone provides. In the instructions for the healing ministry today which are so clearly set out in James 5:14,15, the first promise which is made effective is that of salvation. "... the prayer of faith will *save* the sick man ..." And that is what I have found. More people have been converted to Christ in this way than in any other way, as far as my experience goes. The healing ministry of the Christian church is essentially evangelistic. It meets sick and worried people at their point of felt need and enables them to find Christ.

APPENDIX TO PART 2

THE BISHOPS AND THE HEALING MINISTRY

IN ORDER OF importance, I profess to be a Christian, an Anglican and an Evangelical. Central to my stance is that I am a churchman, which means, in part, that I am under the authority of my bishop. Far from this being a limitation, it releases me to have my own authority within my membership in the church. It reflects our submission to Christ and "the glorious liberty of the children of God".[1] that results from that. To do only what is right in one's own sight will inevitably lead to confusion and division. As a churchman, it follows that I am directly concerned to know the mind of the Anglican church on the healing ministry.

The mind of the church is expressed in different ways, but never with more moral authority than in the meeting of Anglican archbishops and bishops known as the Lambeth Conference. At this Conference, held at intervals of approximately ten years, all the archbishops and diocesan bishops worldwide gather, under the chairmanship of the Archbishop of Canterbury, for a month-long meeting which reviews the affairs of the church and the issues that currently confront it. The report or encyclical letter that they produce and issue at the end of the Conference for the guidance of the church has as its premise: "It has seemed good to the Holy Spirit and to us..."[2]

The Lambeth Conference's deliberations on the healing ministry began in 1908 and have led, directly and indirectly, to various movements within the Anglican church and beyond that have promoted this ministry over the years.

A committee appointed by the 1920 Conference said, "Within the church... systems of healing based on the redemptive work of our Lord... all spring from a belief in the fundamental principle that the power to exercise spiritual healing is taught by Christ to be a natural heritage of Christian people who are living in fellowship with God, and is part of the ministry of Christ through his body the church." [3]

The Conference meeting in 1930 affirmed that the laying on of hands and anointing with oil had a direct physical effect on the human body. It also pressed for increased co-operation between doctors and clergy, and for the formation of regular intercessory prayer groups in parishes. [4]

Through the initiative of the renowned Archbishop William Temple, the Churches' Council for Health and Healing was formed in 1944, in order, as the Archbishop put it, to "clarify the message and to educate Christian people by various means to provide knowledge of spiritual healing and fuller co-operation and understanding between doctors and clergy and all those engaged in health in the full sense." [5] The Council saw its purpose and function to include:

To provide a common basis for the healing movements which stand on Christian foundations.

To afford a recognised basis for the co-operation of doctors and clergy in the study and performance of their respective functions in the work of healing, and to promote this co-operation in thought and action throughout the country.

To bring the work of healing into close relation with the regular work of the churches. [6]

The Archbishops of Canterbury and York set up a

Commission on the Ministry of Healing, which was to report its findings prior to the 1958 Lambeth Conference. The report included the following passage: "The church as the body of Christ is charged with a commission to heal the sick. By evoking the response of faith, the pastoral and sacramental ministry of the church allows the Divine Grace to act creatively and so determine the issue of health in ways beyond our present scientific methods of measurement."[7]

The most recent Lambeth Conference (1978) unanimously passed the following resolution:

The Conference praises God for the renewal of the Ministry of Healing within the churches in recent times and re-affirms:
that the healing of the sick in his name is as much part of the proclamation of the kingdom as the preaching of the good news of Jesus Christ;

that to neglect this aspect of ministry is to diminish our part in Christ's total redemptive activity;

that the ministry to the sick should be an essential element in any revision of the liturgy."[8]

This strong and unequivocal statement is the end result of the research and development of this ministry in the Anglican church over this century, and gives firm and plain guidance for Anglicans to follow.

In the "revision of the liturgy" as seen in the new Australian Prayer Book that has been produced and is used by the Anglican Church of Australia, admirable provision has been made for this ministry. It imparts confidence and encouragement to know that the prayers and liturgical forms used in the healing service in St Andrew's Cathedral, Sydney, and wherever else they are employed, are what our church in Australia provides and authorises through its Prayer Book. And this confidence and encouragement is multiplied when it is remembered that

this provision also reflects the mind of our archbishops
and bishops worldwide as expressed through the Lambeth
Conference.

> Lord and heavenly Father,
> the strengthener of those who suffer in body,
>   mind and soul:
> lay your healing hand on your servant
> that he may be restored to health
> and show his thankfulness in love to you
> and service to his fellows,
> through Jesus Christ our Lord.[9]

REFERENCES

Part 1

Chapter 1
1. 1 John 4:18 (A.V.)
2. Matthew 6:10
3. Luke 10:17–19
4. 1 John 3:8
5. John 19:30
6. Revelation 11:15
7. Luke 17:21
8. 2 Peter 1:4
9. Romans 10:9
10. John 14:12
11. Matthew 6:20
12. Matthew 6:30,31,33
13. 2 Corinthians 11:24–27
14. 2 Corinthians 1:8–9
15. 2 Corinthians 12:7
16. Romans 8:28 (A.V.)
17. 2 Corinthians 1:9 (Phillips)
18. 1 John 4:18
19. James 5:15 (N.I.V.)
20. 2 Corinthians 5:7
21. Hebrews 11:1
22. John 16:15

Chapter 2
1. John 5:6
2. Matthew 12:20
3. *Inner Balance*, ed. by Elliott M. Goldwag, p. 29, Prentice-Hall Inc.

4. ibid., p. 121
5. ibid., p. 47
6. Luke 6:27-29
7. Matthew 5:24
8. 1 Thessalonians 5:18
9. 2 Corinthians 5:17
10. *Realities*, Basilea Schlink, p. 27, Oliphants
11. Matthew 9:29
12. Mark 9:23
13. Matthew 17:20
14. Acts 14:9
15. Hebrews 11:1
16. Matthew 28:20
17. Revelation 3:20
18. Matthew 7:21
19. James 1:27
20. Luke 19:17,19,24
21. Copyright Anglican Church of Australia Trust Corporation. From the text of *An Australian Prayer Book*, published by A.I.O. Reproduced with permission.
22. Mark 11:25,26
23. Philippians 3:13
24. 1 Corinthians 14:40
25. 2 Corinthians 3:17
26. Mark 4:28
27. Colossians 4:2

Chapter 3

1. Matthew 9:29
2. James 5:15 (N.I.V.)
3. Matthew 17:20 (Amp.)
4. Romans 15:13
5. Romans 7:19
6. Colossians 4:2 (A.V.)
7. Philippians 1:6
8. James 1:4
9. *The Power to Heal*, Francis MacNutt, pp. 12/34, Bantam Books Inc.

10. *A History of the Church of England*, M.W. Patterson, p. 108, Longmans and Co.
11. 2 Corinthians 5:17

Part 2

Chapter 4
1. 2 Peter 1:4
2. 1 Corinthians 14:29
3. Ephesians 2:21
4. Ephesians 4:3
5. 2 Corinthians 5:17

Chapter 5
1. *Book of Common Prayer*

Chapter 6
1. Mark 3:27
2. Matthew 16:19
3. Matthew 12:45
4. Ephesians 5:18
5. Ephesians 6:16
6. *Let the Earth Hear His Voice*, ed. by J.D. Douglas, p. 894, World Wide Publications

Chapter 7
1. James 2:26
2. Matthew 6:33
3. Matthew 4:23
4. Luke 9:2
5. Romans 11:29

Appendix to Part 2
1. Romans 8:21
2. Acts 15:28
3. *The Christian Healing Ministry*, Morris Maddocks, p. 104, S.P.C.K.
4. ibid., p. 104

5. ibid., p. 104
6. ibid., p. 105
7. ibid., p. 106
8. ibid., p. 107
9. Copyright Anglican Church of Australia Trust Corporation. From the text of *An Australian Prayer Book*, published by A.I.O. Reproduced with permission.

Noreen Riols

EYE OF THE STORM

Living in Paris with her French husband and struggling to cope with five children, Noreen Riols could not counter the black despair that dragged her into a nervous breakdown. The discovery of new life in Christ was a fresh and exciting beginning, but her faith was to be tested in the continuing ups and downs of family life.

'Little by little I learned that being a Christian is not an insurance policy against pain, that Christ does not take us out of the storms of life, but he does give us his strong hand to hold and his peace in the midst of them.'

Seeing the power of God at work in the miraculous healing of her husband, Noreen testifies to a loving God who can make all things new. Her story will charm, move and encourage.

Francis MacNutt

THE PRAYER THAT HEALS

'Praying at home is such a beautiful experience, and so easy to learn if people are taught and encouraged to try.

I would like this book to help in a gentle revolution that will get families actually to pray together. I hope it will show how you can pray for healing with your husband, your wife, your child, or your friend.'

Francis MacNutt, internationally respected authority on renewal and healing, is author of HEALING and THE POWER TO HEAL.

Jim Glennon

YOUR HEALING IS WITHIN YOU

'The most significant book on healing to come out of the spiritual renewal in the church today. It not only has a sound Scriptural basis but builds faith in the reader and shows him how to appropriate his healing in Christ.'

Colin Urquhart

In this first book on healing, Canon Glennon discusses its different aspects – the prayer of faith, healing the memories, relations with the medical profession – and reviews the healing ministry in the New Testament. He believes that Christian healing is central to Christian ministry.

'This book is strong stuff and we do well to ponder and be challenged by it.'

Church of England Newspaper